THE STORM BEFORE THE CALM

MAKING SENSE OF LIFE'S TROUBLES

THE STORM BEFORE THE CALM

MAKING SENSE OF LIFE'S TROUBLES

TALBOT DAVIS

Scripture quotations unless noted otherwise are from the Common English Bible. Copyright © 2011 by the Common English Bible. All rights reserved. Used by permission. *www.CommonEnglishBible.com.*

Scripture quotations marked (NIV) are taken from the Holy Bible, New International Version®, NIV®. Copyright © 1973, 1978, 1984, 2011 by Biblica, Inc.™ Used by permission of Zondervan. All rights reserved worldwide. *www.zondervan.com.* The "NIV" and "New International Version" are trademarks registered in the United States Patent and Trademark Office by Biblica, Inc.™

Scripture quotations marked (NASB) are taken from the New American Standard Bible®, Copyright © 1960, 1962, 1963, 1968, 1971, 1972, 1973, 1975, 1977, 1995 by The Lockman Foundation. Used by permission. (*www.Lockman.org*)

Library of Congress Cataloging-in-Publication Data

Davis, Talbot.
    The storm before the calm : making sense of life's troubles / Talbot Davis. — 1st [edition].
        pages cm
    ISBN 978-1-5018-0431-1 (binding: pbk.)   1.   Suffering—Religious aspects—Christianity. 2. Consolation. 3. Storms—Biblical teaching. I. Title.
    BV4909.D377 2015
    248.8'6—dc23

                                                            2015023235

15 16 17 18 19 20 21 22 23 24—10 9 8 7 6 5 4 3 2 1
MANUFACTURED IN THE UNITED STATES OF AMERICA

To Julie,
who saw this a long time
before I did.

CONTENTS

INTRODUCTION

The Storm Before the Calm

Storms.

They shake us.

They soak us.

They scare us.

But what if they did something more? What if the real outcome of storms is to prepare us . . . for the calm that follows?

Rather than the usual mindset of "the calm before the storm"—a mindset that sees calm as the exception and storms as the norm—I want to approach the subject from a very different angle in this book.

Calm can—and should—be our life's experience.

Each of the chapters you will read takes a look at some of the best-known storm stories in Scripture, ranging from the two builders of Jesus' parable, to the frightened disciples in the boat with the Savior, to Isaiah's praise of God as a storm shelter, to Paul's shipwreck in Malta, and ultimately to Noah's embarrassing episode after the storm to end all storms in Genesis 9.

I'm constantly amazed at how deeply people resonate with the imagery and metaphor of storms. Perhaps it is because they are so vivid and universal—as I wrote these words in December 2014, Northern California was being assaulted by a powerful, rare storm system they call the Pineapple Express.

My own city of Charlotte was devastated in 1989 by Hurricane Hugo—a storm so freakish in intensity that it actually grew stronger as it headed inland. Ten years later, the eastern part of our state suffered even greater misery as Hurricane Floyd brought widespread flooding to low-lying areas.

And of course, with everyone else in the United States, I watched with helplessness in 2005 as Hurricane Katrina made us wonder, *Will New Orleans ever come back?*

The imagery of storms sticks with us. It becomes easy to transfer the concept of meteorological assault to human difficulty in individual lives and communities.

As you'll read in Chapter 1, all of us are in one of three places:

Emerging out of a storm,
in the eye of the storm,
or headed for a storm.

And these personal storms take so many shapes and forms, including divorce, depression, mental illness, ministry failure, wayward children, and wandering souls.

Those may be the storms of your past, your present, or your future.

As you engage these chapters either individually or with your small group, I believe they will help you navigate the storms in which you find yourself, prepare for the ones to come, and, perhaps most importantly, ensure that you don't chase down and create storms of your own.

Along the way, I invite you to enter into the library of Scripture and all the ways the inspired authors incorporated storms into their stories, from the archetypal storm of Noah and the Flood, to the actual storm that caused Paul's shipwreck, to the representative of storm that assaulted Jesus' "builders" in Luke 6.

These messages were delivered in real time to a real congregation: Good Shepherd United Methodist Church, a modern and multiethnic gathering of souls in Charlotte, North Carolina, who are (a) patient with my sermons and (b) committed to our mission of inviting all people into a living relationship with Jesus Christ.

I have designed this study for individual or group use. At the conclusion of each chapter, I have included "Questions for Reflection and Discussion," a weekly focus, and recommended daily Scripture readings.

So ... storm away. Just recognize your storms may well be but a prelude for the enduring calm where God wants you to stay.

Talbot Davis

THE EYE OF THE STORM

When the flood came, the rising water smashed against that house, but the water couldn't shake the house because it was well built. (Luke 6:48)

Some time ago, Frank Knox, who was then U.S. Secretary of the Navy, uttered the following words:

"Whatever happens, the U.S. Navy is not going to be caught napping."[1]

When did Secretary Knox say this? December 4, 1941: three days before the Japanese attacked the U.S. Navy at Pearl Harbor. Sadly and tragically, the Japanese forces caught the Navy napping.

A storm came in the form of Japanese bombers, fighters, and aircraft carriers, resulting in over 2,400 Americans killed and more than 1,100 wounded. A storm came, and despite boasts to the contrary, there was little preparation and much napping. And the results were predictably tragic.

As we move through this book, particularly here in Chapter 1, "The Eye of the Storm," it will become clear that preparation is important. The message of this chapter, and of the Scripture passage that we will discuss, has everything to do with preparation (or a lack of preparation) and storms. In Luke 6:48-49, Jesus tells the story of two men who each encounter a flood. One man is prepared, and the other is not. One person's house survives the flood, while the other's is swept away. Like the U.S. Navy at Pearl Harbor, the second man is caught napping. Jesus' story vividly illustrates the disaster that can come when we fail to prepare. Yet as we will see, like most of Jesus' parables, it communicates something deeper than the story itself. The tale of the two houses shows us how vital it is to obey Jesus' teachings.

Here is the story, in Luke 6:46-49:

> Why do you call me "Lord, Lord" and don't do what I say? I'll show what it's like when someone comes to me, hears my words, and puts them into practice. It's like a person building a house by digging deep and laying the foundation on bedrock. When the flood came, the rising water smashed against that house, but the water couldn't shake the house because it was well built. But those who don't put into practice what they hear are like a person who built a house without a foundation. The floodwater smashed against it and it collapsed instantly. It was completely destroyed.

Before we look closely at this parable, it's important to recognize when and why Jesus tells it. It occurs at the end of Luke 6, and Jesus uses it to conclude his Sermon on the Plain (Luke 6:17-49). This is Luke's version of Jesus' most famous public address, more widely known as the Sermon on the Mount. It's most commonly called the Sermon on the Mount based on Matthew's version (Matthew 5–7), where Jesus speaks on a mountain (Matthew 5:1). In Luke it's called the Sermon on the Plain because Luke 6:17 tells us that Jesus speaks from "a large area of level ground." It's possible that Matthew and Luke just placed the same sermon at two different locales. Or it's possible that Jesus gave the same basic message at two different times and two different venues. It was important teaching, and he may have delivered it to more than one audience. And here's a little preacher secret: We do that from time to time. "It worked once, so I'm going to give it to this group over here next!"

In either case, the contents of the sermon are some of Jesus' most important and well-known teachings. He gives the sermon near the outset of his public ministry, almost like an outline of the vision of the kingdom of God he will proclaim and exemplify. The Sermon on the Plain, or the Sermon on the Mount, is an important proclamation. And Jesus concludes the sermon with a story of two men, two houses, and a flood.

PREACHERS TAKE CONCLUSIONS VERY SERIOUSLY.

Now, I have preached a few sermons in my day, and here is something I can tell you from experience: Preachers take their conclusions very seriously. We put a lot of thought into how we tie things up and bring the sermon to a close. The ending is the last thing the audience will hear, so it had better be memorable and important. And in the Sermon on the Plain, this story of two men and two houses is Jesus' conclusion. It's his finale. He has taught a lot of deep, important things in the Sermon on the Plain, and this story is his conclusion that brings it all home.

Jesus puts the story of the two men and the storm at the end because he really wants his hearers to remember it. That's a clue that we need to pay close attention. Jesus wants us to be like one of the people in his story and to avoid being like the other person. Like most of the stories Jesus tells, the tale of the two men is about more than just the two men. It starts with curiosity, a pained question from Jesus himself (Luke 6:46):

> Why do you call me "Lord, Lord" and don't do what
> I say?

In other words, why do you want my blessing without obedience? Why do you want all the benefits of following me without following me? Why do you want to boast about me but not surrender to me? Why do you throw my name around but don't let my Spirit shape who you are?

It simply doesn't work that way. We don't really believe it until we actually do what Jesus commands. When it comes to Jesus, what comes out of our mouths doesn't really matter until our actions back it up.

"Why do you call me 'Lord, Lord' and don't do what I say?" I don't think this is the only time Jesus asked this question. I think it was something he must have asked many times. I think it's something he asks of us even today.

Jesus wants us to come to him, hear his words, and then put them into practice (Luke 6:47). And to help us get there, Jesus moves into the story about these two men, both of whom are in home-building mode.

The second man, in verse 49, chooses the easier route for building a home in those days (long before county inspectors!): He builds it without a foundation. In Matthew's Gospel, it says the man builds his house on the sand (Matthew 7:26). Either way, from the start it looks like a questionable building decision. It's actually not quite as absurd as we might think. In that climate, the sand was packed hard in the summer and by all appearances was a solid surface on which to build. And it would have given the man a quick turnaround for completing his home. You can almost imagine the real estate agent saying, "I can have you in by June."

But then a storm happens, and the results speak for themselves. What happens to this quick-build home when the inevitable storm hits? Look at Luke 6:49:

The floodwater smashed against it and it collapsed instantly. It was completely destroyed.

Two words capture it all: *instantly* and *completely*. The house took about as long to fall as it took to build. Destruction was immediate and absolute. Because there was no foundation, everything came crashing down the instant difficulties arrived.

Many of us know this from experience. When we opt for the easy way, collapse is often sudden and thorough. Maybe you know just what happens when you choose the soft and expedient path because you have lived it. Perhaps you kept all the money you made and didn't give to God. Maybe you kept asking, "What's in it for me?" instead of "What will advance God's kingdom?" Or perhaps you knew everything about all the candidates on *American Idol* and nothing about the letters of Paul. Maybe you married mostly for looks. These are shallow values many of us pursue instead of digging deeply into the life Jesus calls us to live. And when the storm comes—for it will come—destruction is swift and sad. This, Jesus says, is what it's like for all those who hear his words and don't put them into practice.

The first man in Jesus' story is different. Look at verses 47-48:

> I'll show what it's like when someone comes to me,
> hears my words, and puts them into practice. It's like
> a person building a house by digging deep and laying
> the foundation on bedrock.

This man lives Jesus' words. For the type of faith God calls us to, there's no difference between believing and obeying. We only believe in Jesus to the extent that we do what he says and follow what he teaches. And when we put Jesus' words into practice, we are like the man who builds his house on a firm foundation. He believes, and so he does. To do this takes a great deal more time and effort and strength. Such a person digs, bores, pours, and then he builds. It's not flashy and it's not easy. It's not a spiritual high. It takes a long time, and it gets repetitive after a while. But the man digs deep and lays a firm foundation, putting in the work to build his house with strength. So it is with those who live by Jesus' words: not just believing them or talking about them, but living them—putting the words into practice.

So what happens to this man and his house? Look at the second part of verse 48:

> When the flood came, the rising water smashed against that house, but the water couldn't shake the house because it was well built.

Those are powerful words. Not only did the house hold on, enduring and avoiding complete destruction. The water couldn't even shake it—*could not shake*. The man and his home didn't just survive the storm; it almost seems as if they were stronger after it than they were before it. The storm passed, and the house was still standing firm. It was unshakable. Of course, the storm wasn't what made the house strong; it just revealed the deep strength that was there all along because of the man's preparation and diligence.

You know what that means? **What you prepare for, you'll prevail over.**

When you prepare, you'll prevail in such a way that your faith, your home, and your spirit all seem stronger as a result of the storm. The storm will reveal who you already are. It will reveal someone who is not just playing at the game of Christian but rather has a living relationship with Jesus Christ.

There's something else that stands out to me in this story, a small detail that makes a huge difference. It's the little word *when* in verse 48: *When the flood came*...

Not if. *When.*

Jesus doesn't talk about *if* the storm comes. He doesn't say *in case* it comes. He says *when* it comes. Stormy seasons in life are inevitable. It's the same for you as it was for the two men. No matter what your circumstances, you are in one of three places:

You just came through a storm.

You are in the middle of a storm right now.

You are headed toward a storm at some point in the future.

WHAT YOU PREPARE FOR, YOU'LL PREVAIL OVER.

We are all in one of these three situations, with a storm of some kind in our past, present, or future. It may be a self-inflicted storm, or it may come from forces beyond your control. Turmoil takes many forms. It can be the job you lose. It can be the marriage that ends or that continues without much love or life. It can be when the doctor gives you or one you love the diagnosis no one wants to hear. Storms will come. It's a matter of *when,* not *if.*

Storms are inevitable. And if you're in the calm, now is the time to prepare for the storm. Prevailing over it can't be separated from preparing for it. When the storms come, that's not the time to become religious. It won't work. You can't suddenly get religious when the job disappears, the marriage collapses, or the diagnosis comes, then overcome your obstacles. You won't have the wherewithal, the spiritual maturity, or the strength of spine. You won't have a foundation to stand on.

Yes, there exceptions to this. Sometimes a "crisis faith" ends up working in the long run. But you can't count on that because more often than not, it doesn't work. Usually a crisis faith disappears as soon as the crisis goes away. Or the type of faith that is cultivated in those moments is too weak to withstand the storm in the first place. Storms have an uncanny way of revealing what's already there in your spiritual life.

THE STORMS OF LIFE EXPOSE WHAT'S ALREADY GOING ON INSIDE OF YOU.

That bears repeating: The storms of life, better than anything else, expose what's already going on inside of you spiritually.

And my great longing—since storms are not an *if* but a *when*—is that when storms hit you, they will reveal someone who has dug deeply into Jesus.

It's a bit like a test that psychologists conducted a number of years ago that involved four-year-old children and marshmallows. In the test, they would put a four-year-old in a room with a marshmallow. The interviewer would tell the child, "I'm going to run an errand, but I will leave this marshmallow while I'm gone. You can have it now…but if you wait until I return, you can have two!" Then the interviewer would leave the child alone to observe him or her from another room. As expected, some of the children waited, and others ate the marshmallow right away.

The people conducting the test tracked the children as they grew, measuring their behavior in various ways. Eventually they discovered that the ones who waited, who delayed their gratification so they could get two marshmallows instead of just one, scored an average of 210 points higher on the SAT than those who ate the one marshmallow right away. There is value to steady, patient, discipline in the calm. *What you prepare for, you'll prevail over.*

Or it's like Rosa Parks. Legend would have us believe that when she refused to give up her seat on the bus, it was a spontaneous, unplanned, spur-of-the-moment decision. But that wasn't quite the case. She was not old or physically tired. But she was tired of giving in, and she had within her a spirit of courage and determination that she would no longer endure being treated as a lesser human being. Because she had a strong foundation based in part on her faith, she was able to be steadfast and immovable when the storm swirled on that day. And she was unshaken by the rising flood that followed from her actions. *What you prepare for, you'll prevail over.*

Or it's like the testimony I received from a woman at Good Shepherd Church:

> We all walk the road of preparation whether we recognize it or not prior to our storms. Back in 2006, I stayed home from work one day due to the flu. Because of a broadcast I watched that day, I decided to put into place some spiritual disciplines that I never had before. I began praying to God first thing in the morning and studying His word daily. I knew the only way to really get to know Him was to spend time with Him in addition to church. I knew that there would be something powerful about private worship that would bring me closer to Him.
>
> Through these wonderful disciplines, God's spirit touched mine in February of 2006 beckoning something deeper from me. When God gently nudged me toward Him I felt my spiritual life growing. Little did I know the adversities I would face later that year. When God originally placed on my heart His desire to draw me closer, I thought it was for Him. Now I understand it was to prepare and grow me towards

total dependence on Him to guide me through the darkness. He didn't "need" anything from me—He knew I would "need" from Him.

My father was diagnosed with a terminal illness that year and my sister a year later. Over the next three years, I had to watch both of them die. Over and over He showed me that entering into His strength would only occur when I exited out of my own. Through Scripture and prayer, I have learned that I do not have to know where He is taking me as long as I have peace in the One who is leading me.

My heart spills over with sincere gratitude when I think of what the journey would have looked like without the road of preparation He placed me on in 2006. He still gives me grace portions in the measurements just right for me as I have learned to live without my father and my sister. His grace never fails!

Here's what I've come to believe. A lot of folks come to church to have their ears tickled. This is especially true for a church like Good Shepherd where the experience and presentation are pretty good. A lot of folks come to church to hear and see some cool stuff and then come back the next week for some more. But they don't come with the intention of *applying* any of it.

They come to *hear* but *not apply*.

It's been that way for a long, long time, because Jesus was addressing it among his earliest followers. That's the whole point of his story about the two men and their houses and the storm. Even in his own day, there were people who came to hear Jesus' words but didn't put them into practice. And the results are the same now as they were back then. Hearing the words but not living them out is a recipe for disaster when the inevitable storms come. You know if it's you that Jesus is talking about here:

"Oh, the Bible's too hard to read."

"I don't have time to pray."

"I can barely pay the bills even before giving to God."

"I'll forgive her as long as she changes her ways."

You know if it's you. Or rather, you know where and how these words are true in your life. In Luke 6:46, Jesus asks all of us, *Why do you call me "Lord, Lord" and don't do what I say?* We're the ones Jesus asks about in Luke 6, because we all have some parts of our lives where we're content to hear Jesus' words and stop there. And when the storms come, we might be caught napping rather than prepared.

But on the flip side, when someone prepares in the calm, it's a glorious thing. When the storms come and reveal a deep, living faith rather than shallow ear tickling, it's beautiful.

To those people—prepared people—the storm seems like a drizzle. Have you noticed that? I know I have. Two people can respond to the same situation in very different ways. One responds with panic and meltdown, the other with a sense of eerie calm. For one person it seems like a disastrous flood, but for another person it's like a light rain. And the difference is the kind of disciples we have allowed God to make us into. *What you prepare for, you'll prevail over.*

So…how, then? How do you prepare?

What I'm about to share are not new truths. My role most of the time is not to tell you something new but to remind you of things you already know. There is no magic formula, no quick fix that will automatically turn you into a prepared person. Chasing after something like that would be as foolish as building your house without a foundation. Preparation is about following Jesus in deed as well as in word, obeying his teachings day after day. It's about actually doing the things you already know about and doing them regularly over the long haul.

In some ways, these things make me think of Malcolm Gladwell's *Outliers: The Story of Success,* a popular book about the source of genius. Here's the spoiler: Genius doesn't just happen. The book made it known that genius is less the product of natural gift and more the result of focused effort. What Gladwell found is that ten thousand hours of practice is the threshold of mastery. It takes a minimum of ten thousand hours of practice and work to become truly great at something. It's why the Beatles were such good musicians, and it's why Andre Agassi had an uncanny ability to hit the tennis ball with such precision. (I used to think he was incredibly lucky. But no, he just hit a million more balls than I ever did!)

PREPARATION MEANS FOLLOWING JESUS IN DEED AS WELL AS IN WORD.

So here are some steps you can take to focus on your spiritual life and prepare for the storm:

(1) Get *away* and get *alone*. Get away from people and get alone with your Father. Spend some time with the Bible on your lap and your spirit open to its challenges, followed by a time of prayer. Do this not as an obligation but as a privilege, and practice the privilege with discipline.

(2) Practice *community on purpose*. Surround yourself with like-minded people headed on a similar path. It's not only about you and Jesus! It's about you, Jesus, and the people you share him with.

(3) *Tithe*. Gulp! The best way to prevent money problems is to give God what belongs to him first. Yes! It really is that easy.

(4) Practice *forgiveness* and *not revenge*. That's the thrust of Jesus' sermon in the earlier parts of Luke: Don't retaliate; love your enemies; don't get trapped in cycles of getting even. Think of all the energy that saves!

What you prepare for, you'll prevail over.

There's something else I have to believe is true, even though it's not technically in Jesus' story about the two men in Luke 6. This kind of deep, disciplined preparation will not only enable you to prevail over storms, it will also prevent a lot of them in the first place.

Of course, this kind of living will never prevent all storms. Some of them come as forces beyond our control. But it can help us weather them with grace, beauty, and strength. In 2013, a woman at Good Shepherd Church was diagnosed with pancreatic cancer. She was given two weeks to live, and she died ten days into that. And it was one of the best things that happened in our church community that year. Why would I say such a thing, that a sudden death from cancer was one of the best things there? Because ... well, have you ever seen a beautiful death? This one was. The woman knew where she was going and that God would be there with her every step of the way. She had a softness and a glow about her, an anticipation that stayed even as she got sicker. Because of years and years of faith, she knew the promise of 2 Corinthians 5:8 would be hers: "We are confident, and we would prefer to leave the body and to be at home with the Lord."

She didn't *become* that serene in the storm that swirled around her. The storm *revealed* her inner peace, which she had cultivated through many years of living faith.

She could prevail because she had prepared. May that be true of you as well.

What you prepare for, you'll prevail over.

Questions for Reflection and Discussion

Write responses and other thoughts in the space below each question. If you are discussing the book in a small group, prepare for the meeting by writing answers in advance.

1. Recall the most recent storm you endured in life. What happened? How did you respond? What did the storm reveal?

2. Think of someone you know who has endured life's storms well. What seems to be the reason for that person's ability to endure?

3. Have you had experience with "crisis faith"? Have you seen it in others? What characteristics tend to define or accompany such a faith?

4. What does a deep, faith-filled life look like to you? What are the main attributes? What are its effects on a person?

5. This week's daily Scripture readings include both instances of the Sermon on the Mount/Plain in Matthew 5–7 and Luke 6. In the space below, list similarities in the two versions of this sermon. Now list the differences.

6. Which one would you rather have heard in person—the Sermon on "the Mount" or the one on "the Plain"? Why?

7. What are some ways you are preparing for your next storm?

8. How would you evaluate the foundation on which you are building your "home"? Is it more rock or sand?

9. Think about the relationships in your life, the people with whom you spend the most time. In what ways are they helping you to build a strong foundation of spiritual preparation?

10. Starting today, what can you do to dig deeply and lay a firm foundation of a living, active faith?

Work on Your Foundation

Spend some regular, purposeful, disciplined time with God this week. You may choose something that you have never done before or something that you already do but would like to do more regularly or with more attention and focus. Read the Bible, pray, fast from a meal, sing a hymn, or identify another spiritual practice that you can do every day. Ideally this will be something you can do at the same time each day. As you do, remember that you are working on your foundation, putting time and energy into your relationship with God.

Closing Prayer

Eternal God, stir in our hearts and move us to prepare by digging deeply into you. Give us a hunger for time alone with you. Give us companions who build us up as we follow you together. Give us generosity to give of our time and our possessions to others. And give us grace to sow peace rather than seek revenge when we are wronged. We know that storms will come. But we also know that when you are our foundation, we will prevail. Amen.

Daily Scripture Readings

This week, read the following Scripture passages. As you read, ask how God is calling you to put Jesus' words into practice and live by them.

Monday: Luke 6:17-49
Tuesday: Matthew 5:1–6:34
Wednesday: Matthew 7:1-29
Thursday: Proverbs 6:1-11
Friday: Proverbs 10:1-10

1. From *http://www.quote-wise.com/quotes/author/frank-knox*.

2

STORM CHASERS

Overcome with awe, they said to each other, "Who then is this? Even the wind and the sea obey him!" (Mark 4:41)

A long, long time ago, maybe even in a galaxy far, far away, I took my very first preaching class in seminary. I think I took about four all together. You only had to take one, but I guess I was a remedial student. That first one was with a professor whom I absolutely loved and still do. But one day during the semester, he did something unexpected. Out of nowhere, he read us the story of Jesus calming the storm in the Gospel of Mark. Jesus and the disciples are in a boat on the Sea of Galilee when a storm threatens to sink their vessel. Jesus, however, commands the storm to stop, and the weather becomes calm.

After reading it to us, he said, "Here's an outline for you for a sermon on that passage: *Great Storm, Great Christ, Great Calm.*" Catchy! I still remember it twenty-five years later. And so, when it was time to deliver the second "Storm Before the Calm" sermon at Good Shepherd, I almost went ahead and delivered that sermon: Great Storm, Great Christ, Great Calm. I almost used that three-part outline, even though I rarely preach three-point sermons anymore. The neat phrasing and simple outline seemed memorable enough that it was worth deviating from the norm.

I almost prepared that sermon…except—despite my enduring love for that professor—that's not what the story is really about. There's not a tidy bow around it here in the Gospel of Mark. It may be the best storm story of them all, but it's not as straightforward as that simple three-part formula leads you to believe. It is in fact much more interesting than that. And when we dig into the story, we see that it's really a story of storm *chasers* with a remarkable twist at the end. Here's the full story, in Mark 4:35-41:

> Later that day, when evening came, Jesus said to them, "Let's cross over to the other side of the lake." They left the crowd and took him in the boat just as he was. Other boats followed along.
>
> Gale-force winds arose, and waves crashed against the boat so that the boat was swamped. But Jesus was in the rear of the boat, sleeping on a pillow. They woke him up and said, "Teacher, don't you care that we're drowning?"
>
> He got up and gave orders to the wind, and he said to the lake, "Silence! Be still!" The wind settled down and there was a great calm. Jesus asked them, "Why are you frightened? Don't you have faith yet?"
>
> Overcome with awe, they said to each other, "Who then is this? Even the wind and the sea obey him!"

Now here's what you need to know as we plunge into Mark's storm story: The disciples should have known better than to let Jesus convince them to go out on the boat that day. Look at verses 35 and 36: Jesus suggests that he and the disciples should go to the other side of the lake, and they say yes. They even got other boats to join them! But as I said, they should have known better. Why?

THE DISCIPLES SHOULD HAVE KNOWN BETTER.

Well, many of the disciples were from Galilee, and at least four of them—Simon (Peter), Andrew, James, and John—were fishermen who made their living in and on the Sea of Galilee. The Sea of Galilee was their lifeblood, and they knew its secrets, its contours, and its patterns as well as they knew their own souls. And because of its unique topography, the Sea of Galilee is subject to sudden, severe, and violent winds.

The Sea of Galilee—which, if you look for it on a modern map, is now called Lake Kinneret—sits at a low elevation, actually about two hundred meters below sea level. It is the lowest body of freshwater in the world. It's not lower than the Dead Sea (which is saltwater), but it's still very low. And much higher elevations surround it, including mountains and the Golan Heights, an area that appears on the news these days as a flashpoint in Palestinian–Israeli conflicts. So the lake sits in this low bowl, and it's fed by both the Jordan River and hot springs. Because of its unique shape and surroundings, the Sea of Galilee can become a cauldron for violent weather, with cold air meeting hot water and winds funneling onto it from the mountainous regions nearby.

The disciples might not have known the meteorological and geographical science behind the Sea of Galilee, but as fishermen who had grown up on its shores, they would have surely known the warning of an impending storm. At the very least, they would have recognized the conditions that made a storm more likely than at other times. And with that lifetime of firsthand knowledge, the disciples could have informed Jesus about it when he suggested they go to the other side of the lake. They could have—should have—said to Jesus, "Not so fast, our Nazarene friend. It's not safe. Maybe tomorrow."

But they didn't. Instead, the disciples agreed to Jesus' suggestion and took him across the lake in a boat. Sure enough, while they were on the lake that night, a storm arose:

> Gale-force winds arose, and waves crashed against the boat so that the boat was swamped. (Mark 4:37)

A storm came about, with fierce winds and violent waves. This was not just any storm; it was a relentless, gale-force windstorm that threatened to sink their boat. Look again at that last detail of verse 37: "Waves crashed against the boat so that the boat was swamped." That paints a vivid picture. The disciples can't keep up with the waves; the more they bail water, the more water pours onboard. The winds keep blowing, and they are just about to be capsized. The hits come faster than the relief.

SOMETIMES THE HITS COME FASTER THAN THE RELIEF.

That's the way life can be sometimes, isn't it? Waves pour in on life, putting you on the verge of going under. You do your best to stay afloat, bailing the water out and dealing with problems as they come, but they keep coming harder and faster than you can handle. Some of you know exactly what that is like.

That's what it's like when your spouse leaves…
> when you discover that your child does drugs…
> when you realize that your sibling has an eating disorder…
> when your car breaks down the same month you have an emergency medical bill…
> when you mom tells you she has cancer…
> when the doctor tells you that *you* have cancer…

At times like these, and many others, the waves break over you faster than you can bail the water out. As you read about the disciples on the lake in the middle of the storm, you know what these guys were going through.

As the disciples furiously bailed water, where was Jesus? He was "in the rear of the boat, sleeping on a pillow." The disciples woke him up and asked him, "Teacher, don't you care that we're drowning?" (4:38).

"TEACHER, DON'T YOU CARE?"

You know that question too, don't you? Sometimes when you're bailing out water, just trying to survive and keep yourself from sinking, it seems like Jesus is asleep. It feels like he's doing nothing to help, and you might as well be on your own. And you want to scream at Jesus just like the disciples did: "Don't you care?!" You've felt that. I've felt it. When parents get divorced, sickness goes unhealed, bills go unpaid, we shake our fists at the sleeping Lord. "What about me?" we ask. We've heard of Jesus doing good things for others and wonder why he's sleeping in our boat instead of helping out. "Don't you care?" is just another way of saying, "Wake up, will you!? It's a storm and I need you desperately!" And that urgent cry leads to Jesus' response in verse 39:

> He got up and gave orders to the wind, and he said
> to the lake, "Silence! Be still!" The wind settled down
> and there was a great calm.

Jesus never answers the disciples' question. This is the first of three unanswered questions we see in this passage. Instead, Jesus gets up. Evidently, the disciples' voices awaken him when the storm does not. And when he gets up, he doesn't address the disciples directly; he speaks instead to the wind and the waves. Jesus tells the storm, "Silence! Be still!" And the storm does. Jesus stops the storm. This tells me that he probably sent it in the first place, but I can't prove that. All I know is that with a simple command, "Silence! Be still!" the storm stops immediately. And when he stops it, the result is *complete, thorough, and eerie calm.*

When Jesus commands the storm, he doesn't speak directly to the disciples. But I do think he means for them to overhear his words. I think he means for them to quiet their own fears and be still. And after the storm stops, Jesus does turn to his disciples. He asks them the second of three unanswered questions in this passage:

> Jesus asked them, "Why are you frightened? Don't
> you have faith yet?" (Mark 4:40)

In other words, why do you not recognize that my presence is enough in any storm? Why are your circumstances more real to you than your Savior? I knew a woman once who was struggling with cancer. Demonstrating great faith in Jesus, she told me, "Wherever I'm going, he's already there." Jesus wants that kind of faith in his followers, and he's not seeing it among the guys with him on the boat. In asking why they are frightened, he's pointing out that they have nothing to fear. In asking whether they have faith yet, he implies that they don't. As I said, this is the second unanswered question. The disciples don't reply to Jesus.

And now here comes that twist at the end I told you about. The disciples don't answer Jesus, but they do ask a question among themselves:

> Overcome with awe, they said to each other, "Who then is this? Even the wind and the sea obey him!" (Mark 4:41)

That's the third unanswered question in this passage: "Who then is this?" Even the wind and the waves obey Jesus' commands. Who is this guy? That's the central question in the entire Gospel of Mark: *Who is Jesus?* Not just this chapter, but the whole book wrestles with this question. Much of Mark's literary genius is in the way he gradually reveals to the characters in the story what the readers have known all along: Jesus is the Son of God. So in looking at Mark 4:35-41, we who read know something that those who sail do not: Jesus is not just a "teacher" (verse 38), but the One who is in charge of the winds and the sea.

But the twist comes before their question, in the first part of verse 41: The disciples were "overcome with awe." Other translations say, "They were terrified" (NIV), or "They became very much afraid" (NASB), which is a more accurate way to understand what happened. Mark uses stronger language here than he ever used to describe the disciples' feelings about the storm. Mark implies that the disciples were afraid during the storm, and Jesus asks why they were "frightened." But after the storm, they were *terrified*. That language is not accidental; it's strategic! After the storm is when the disciples are most scared of all. The real terror happens not when the waves are crashing in the boat but when everything is perfectly quiet and still. There's something about a smooth sea, still air, and an *awake* Jesus that is scarier than the furious, boat-drenching, life-threatening squall while Jesus is asleep.

Here's what Mark is saying in this storm story: ***Sometimes the calm is scarier than the storm.***

SOMETIMES THE CALM IS SCARIER THAN THE STORM.

In the calm, the disciples come face-to-face with the truth of who Jesus is. Without the storm to focus on, without the urgent business to distract them, they confront the reality of Jesus' *identity*. And Jesus' identity is, they realize, infinitely higher and more powerful than they have previously understood. That's what the story is about: Who is Jesus? And when his identity is revealed, even for just that moment, it takes the disciples' breath away. He is the one who has the power to give orders to the wind and the sea. The one who stops the storm might even be the one who sends it in the first place. And if those things are true, it means that "teacher" barely scratches the surface of who Jesus is. If he can stop the storm, he's not a teacher. He's not a great man. He's not a role model. If he can stop the storm, he is God.

The storm story in Mark 4 is not about what Jesus does; it's about who Jesus is. It's not about his performance; it's about his identity. And when you come face-to-face with the truth about who he is, it's a cause for awe, honor, and yes, fear. *Sometimes the calm is scarier than the storm.*

In the storm we can distract ourselves with all our urgent stuff, when what Jesus really wants us to deal with is him. Storms are scary, but we know how to confront them. Even though they might threaten our lives, we at least understand what they are. But how frightening is it to realize, with nothing to distract us, that we're standing right there in front of God? It's one thing to face down the waves with determination and a bucket. It's another matter to stand in a boat with the one who makes the wind blow.

When we come to those seasons in life where we deal more with Jesus' *identity* than his *rescue,* then we have to trust him with the mundane serenity of life. Ironically, what many of us do in that scenario—in the calm, with Jesus and his royal identity looking us square in the face—is that we kick him out of the boat! Here's what I mean: Almost all of us trust him in the storm. When we're desperate is when we get all religious. We come to church. We start to pray. We see a pastor. We open up a Bible. And then...the crisis passes and we revert back to the same casual, occasional faith we had before—the kind of faith where we would prefer to sail solo instead of being confronted with Jesus' annoying, persistent identity as Lord of lords and King of kings. I've seen it a million times.

CAN YOU TRUST JESUS IN THE CALM?

So the real measure of faith is this: Can you trust Jesus in the calm, where there's no crisis, with the *same level of urgency* as you do when it's stormy? Can you love him when his identity is more important than his rescue? It's easy to be desperately religious in the storm. What Jesus is looking for is someone who can be desperately religious in the calm. Can you trust and call on him when your marriage is good? when your kids are healthy? when your bank account is full? Can you acknowledge that you are not in control when you get that promotion? *Everyone* gives their layoff to God. Jesus is looking for folks who give him their prosperity too. *Will you keep Jesus in the boat when the sailing is smooth?*

When the disciples asked Jesus, "Don't you care that we're drowning?" (4:38), he never answered their question. Perhaps he was silent because what he really cared about was what would happen when the storm passed. He had concern over their fate during the storm, but he cared more about *how they lived*. And the same is true for us today. The calm comes, and like the disciples, all of a sudden you don't need Jesus' *answers*. You come face-to-face with Jesus himself. The calm makes you do that. *Sometimes the calm is scarier than the storm.*

The calm is also scary because (get ready for an "ouch"!) when it's calm, it's much harder to complain. And some of us simply cannot be happy unless we have something to complain about! It sounds odd, but it's true. It's why some of us sabotage relationships. It's why we *chase storms*. Remember how the disciples could have and should have told Jesus no instead of getting on the boat? Some of us aren't happy unless we're in a crisis, and—get this—if we're not in a crisis, we'll create one. Secretly, we love the attention and the energy we get from being in the center of a storm, and we'd rather have that than the quiet, calm confrontation with Jesus.

It's why some of you married the wrong guy or gal. It's why others of you keep dating people who are bad for you. It's why you drink the wrong drink, take the wrong risks, confront the wrong sin. It's why you create drama where none exists. Perhaps as you're reading this, some of your issues are coming into focus. "That's why I do what I do! I'm scared of the calm, so I create the storm!"

A friend of mine from Good Shepherd put it this way:

> After my breast cancer diagnosis, when I hit the "calm" part—I was a few years out, the cancer hadn't returned—I would imagine every ache and pain was the cancer returning. I would "manufacture" a storm because I was so accustomed to them. I was living

in a constant state of false fear because I didn't know how to survive the calm. I didn't know what to do with myself, where to turn. I kept waiting for the axe to fall and when it didn't, I "imagined" my way into thinking it was. Even though I longed to live in a "rut," something most people want to escape, I couldn't. I desperately needed peace, but I didn't know how to exist there and so constantly dying was my "go to" home when the calm became too overwhelming. Crazy, huh? Amazing what the human mind will do to escape something, even when it's good for us.

Of course, we don't do this consciously, but often, the more subconscious it is, the more powerful it becomes. When things are going well, we start feeling uneasy, and for some unexplained reason we run off to chase down a storm and make it our own. I know there are people who wake up in the morning and *look* for ways to get offended. They get their feelings hurt a lot. Someone can look back at his or her history of relationships and can identify instance after instance of someone who gave offense in one way or another. But the truth is, there's only one person who is the common denominator in all of those hurt feelings: the one who gets offended so quickly and easily. Because we're so frightened by the calm, we want a storm so badly we'll go looking for one.

Really, most folks handle adversity better than prosperity. It's certainly true in my business! It's staggering how many high-profile pastors find a way to bring things crashing down. They have a kind of influence most of us long for but then blow it all through a moral failure that gets out of control. We can see that in other ways too. Do you know what group of people has among the highest rates of depression, divorce, and discord? Lottery winners! Hello! People are suddenly overwhelmingly wealthy, and in so many instances it ruins their lives. Most of us don't know what to do with such prosperity. A storm ensues because, deep down, that's easier to live with and make sense of than the calm.

Here's the deal: This storm story in Mark 4 is not really about the "Great Storm, Great Christ, Great Calm." It's about *the great fear,* when you're face-to-face with a great Savior and you need to be shaped by his identity more than you need to be sheltered by his rescue. Can you trust God with your everyday life with the same desperation with which you trust him in your storms? If you're one of those storm chasers, will you stop making storms out of whatever is handy?

STOP CHASING STORMS.

I want to invite you to embrace a new pattern today. Instead of making drama, celebrate peace. Instead of sabotaging relationships, give God glory for the ones that are going well.

When you enter that season of prosperity, that's when you need God more than ever—because you're missing that raw desperation that drives you to Christ and drives you to your knees! And if you're in that calm, use that time to gaze upon and trust in the one who fills that calm with his presence and power just as surely as he did the storm.

If you've just now realized you're a storm chaser, then stop! Today! Stop chasing storms and making them your own. For the sake of your family and friends, stop it! For the sake of your own serenity and sanity, stop it! For God's sake, stop it!

Stop chasing storms. Start expecting calm.

Sometimes the calm is scarier than the storm.

Questions for Reflection and Discussion

Write responses and other thoughts in the space below each question. If you are discussing the book in a small group, prepare for the meeting by writing answers in advance.

1. Talk about a time when you wanted to ask Jesus along with the disciples in the boat, "Don't you care?" What was that like?

2. What is your typical response when the hits come faster than the relief (4:37)?

3. The message states that this story is not about Jesus'
    performance; it's about his *identity*. What is the unanswered
    question in 4:41 that leads to that assertion? How do *you*
    answer the question the disciples ask? (To see how Mark
    answers it, read Chapter 5!)

4. Talk about the difficulty of trusting Jesus in the calm. Are
    you more likely to be faithful to him in times of adversity or
    in times of prosperity? Why do you answer as you do?

5. Be honest: Have there been times when you've been so fearful of the calm that you've chased a storm down and made it your own?

6. What happens when you create drama out of thin air?

7. How will you trust him in the calm this week? Be specific.

Stop Chasing Storms

Make a list of three people whom you deeply trust. They may be fellow members of a group study, friends, family members, or some other relationship to you. The important thing is that you value their wisdom and trust them to be honest with you. Sometime this week, describe the truths of this chapter to each of them. Ask each one, "Honestly, do I chase storms?" Then ask, "Do I kick Jesus out of the boat when the sailing is smooth?" Depending on the answers you receive, determine to stop chasing storms and to start trusting Christ in the calm.

Closing Prayer

God, we pray today that you would defeat and demolish our fear of the calm. Instead, give us the ability to trust you with our prosperity and favor. Lead us to trust you with the routine and the mundane. And if any of us chase storms and make them our own, give us the ability to stop and rest in you, enjoying your favor in the calm. Amen.

Daily Scripture Readings

This week, read the following Scripture passages. As you read, pay attention to what makes Jesus scarier than life's storms.

Monday: Mark 4:35-41
Tuesday: Mark 5:1-20
Wednesday: Mark 5:21-43
Thursday: Matthew 14:22-36
Friday: Revelation 1:1-8

3

STORM SHELTERS

You have been a refuge for the poor, a refuge for the needy in distress, a hiding place from the storm, a shade from the heat. (Isaiah 25:4)

I grew up in Dallas, Texas. As you may know, Dallas is at the southern end of Tornado Alley, the region in our country where tornadoes occur most frequently. It's not in the epicenter, like Oklahoma or Kansas, but it's still subject to unpredictable, violent weather. Now, one of the safest places to be in a tornado is underground, but very few houses in Texas have basements. Instead, at least back in the sixties and seventies when I was there, a lot of people had storm shelters out by the side of their houses. When it got scary, you'd open up one of those heavy green metal doors, scoot down the stairs into the small, claustrophobic space, and huddle below. Outside the sky might be heaving and the heavens convulsing, but you'd be below, protected and secure. These Texas storm shelters have never made a single storm disappear or lessen in intensity, but they sure have protected and sheltered a lot of people *during* the storms.

If I've learned anything over my time in ministry, it's that a lot of people find themselves in the middle of storms that they didn't cause, couldn't prevent, and couldn't avoid. Storms like this are going to rage around you regardless of how you respond. If you spend a week in parish ministry, you'll come away with a year's worth of stories about storms and the havoc they cause. They're the kind of storms that you can't just snap your finger and make disappear:

> It's when your teenager tests positive for drugs.

> It's when your *parent* tests positive for drugs.

> It's the friend I know whose wife and sister both died in a short span of time, and all he could say to me was, *"When's it going to stop?"*

> It's the preacher friends I know who won't get on e-mail anymore because they can't handle all the criticism and accusations that flood their inboxes . . . from church members!

Sometimes in the middle of those storms and others, all you want to do is open a trap door and descend into a shelter for a few moments of peace. You know the storm's not going away; you know you can't make it stop right now. But you would give anything for some precious relief in a shelter. That's all you want. It doesn't need to last forever, just a few moments of refuge. The storm is raging all around, but you just need . . . rest . . . time to breathe. You pray not for a miracle to make the storm go away but just for some shelter in the middle of it. I think we've all been there and felt that kind of yearning.

We read in the Scriptures that God provides shelter in times of storm and chaos. Look at one such promise, in the words of Isaiah 25:4:

You have been a refuge for the poor,
a refuge for the needy in his distress,
a hiding place from the storm,
a shade from the heat.

We receive these words like a breath of fresh air. When we read them, we think, *Yes! I knew coming to church and reading the Bible might actually help one day! I knew God would come through!* It's right there on the page: God is a shelter, a hiding place from the storm.

HOW DO YOU GET THESE WORDS OFF THE PAGE AND INTO YOUR HEART?

But then...reality sinks in: Right now, these are just words on a page. In the middle of the storm, your heart drops as you realize, "I'm not *living* these words; I'm merely *reading* them." So how do you get them off the page and into your heart? How can we reduce the distance between what we read and what we live? How can this promise be yours?

As usual, the answers to these questions emerge when we look at the context and setting of this verse in Isaiah 25 and in the whole Book of Isaiah. As I often tell the people of Good Shepherd Church, we need to keep in mind the acronym *C.I.E.*: Context Is Everything. When you take a Scripture passage out of context, it can be confusing or even misleading. But when you read it in its context—that is, its historical and literary setting—the passage becomes clearer and you have a better sense of its meaning. So we need to understand what's going on in the rest of the Book of Isaiah and what was happening during Isaiah's time when he wrote these words.

The Book of Isaiah is an interesting, sometimes confusing, mixture of praises, complaints, songs of worship, and announcements of judgment. The first thirty-nine chapters are set, for the most part, during the late 700's B.C. (Chapters 40–66 are set some 150–200 years later, and many scholars suggest they actually come from a later prophet writing in Isaiah's name.) At this time in the late 700's B.C., the tiny kingdom of Judah was under constant threat of attack and takeover from the Assyrians. The Assyrians were a powerful empire in that area of the world, violently conquering and subjecting the people groups all around them. Not only did they win wars; they did terrible things to the cities and people who rebelled against them in order prevent other cities from doing the same. They impaled their enemies on poles, elevating their bodies for display. They would even put the heads of their enemies on poles, then make the friends and family of the deceased carry these poles around during a victory parade.[1]

CONTEXT IS EVERYTHING.

In other words, the Assyrians were every bit as vicious and inhumane as those who terrorize innocent civilians in the twenty-first century. They were storm troopers. So it's safe to say that Isaiah's people were under constant storm watch as the Assyrian storm threatened their very lives. That was Isaiah's world; that was the historical setting in which the prophet proclaimed the words of Isaiah 25. He envisioned God as a shelter from the awful, inevitable storm known as Assyria.

The surrounding verses in Isaiah 25 give us some clues about what Isaiah meant in describing God as a storm shelter in verse 4.

Reading the rest of Isaiah 25:1-8 will help us see how this promise can be a reality in the midst of our own lives' storms.

LORD, you are my God.
I will exalt you; I will praise your name,
   for you have done wonderful things,
      planned long ago, faithful and sure.
You have turned the city into rubble,
   the fortified town into a ruin,
   the fortress of foreigners into a city no more,
   never to be rebuilt.
Therefore, strong people will glorify you;
   the towns of tyrant nations will fear you.
You have been a refuge for the poor,
   a refuge for the needy in distress,
   a hiding place from the storm,
   a shade from the heat.
When the breath of tyrants is like a winter storm
   or like heat in the desert,
   you subdue the roar of foreigners.
Like heat shaded by a cloud,
   the tyrants' song falls silent.
On this mountain,
   the LORD of heavenly forces will prepare for all peoples
      a rich feast, a feast of choice wines,
     of select foods rich in flavor,
     of choice wines well refined.
He will swallow up on this mountain the veil that is veiling
      all peoples,
   the shroud enshrouding all nations.
He will swallow up death forever.
The LORD God will wipe tears from every face;
   he will remove his people's disgrace from off the whole earth,
     for the LORD has spoken.

In spite of the ruthless storm that surrounds Isaiah's people, he still finds reason to praise God. Why? Look how Isaiah starts this section in verse 1: "LORD, you are my God. I will exalt you; I will praise your name, for you have done wonderful things, planned long ago, faithful and sure." That last part—"wonderful things, planned long ago, faithful and sure"—plants Isaiah squarely in the setting of God's timeline, not his. Isaiah recognizes that God's timeline is eternal, beginning long before Isaiah's day and extending long after it. In part, Isaiah's praise begins with God's timing. Tuck that away because we will come back to it.

In the next verse, we see why Isaiah praises God: "You have turned the city into rubble, the fortified town into a ruin, the fortress of foreigners into a city no more, never to be rebuilt" (Isaiah 25:2). God, the prophet recognizes, ensures the humility and defeat of the strong. Isaiah mentions "the fortress of foreigners," meaning that he is talking about the city or cities of the Assyrians. And God is able to destroy them and bring their strongholds to ruin. All of the human ingenuity and strength—captured by words like *fortified* and *fortress*—are no match for God's power. The Assyrians were powerful and terrifying, but they were nothing in God's eyes. In this case, it seems like God is the storm sender, bringing destruction on Israel's powerful enemies.

Verse 3 tells us why: "Therefore, strong people will glorify you; the towns of tyrant nations will fear you." God tears all that stuff down so that the arrogant, violent invaders will one day be humbled. The enemies, even the Assyrians, will acknowledge that God is King. Those who cause the storms that make God's people suffer will, in the end, recognize God's power.

God is a shelter for the storm. In verses 4-5, we read, "When the breath of tyrants is like a winter storm or like heat in the desert, you subdue the roar of foreigners." The Assyrians, the tyrants, are like a winter storm or the heat of the desert. These ruthless enemies are the storm causers. That detail really jumps out at me because many of us have storm causers in our own lives. In the last chapter, we looked at storm chasers, those who chase down storms of their own making because they are not happy in the calm. But there are others, like the Assyrians, who create storms not for themselves but for other people. Not every storm comes about because of such storm causers, but many do. And some people in our world today, perhaps many people, have these kinds of folks in their lives:

Perhaps you grew up with an abusive parent. And now you've become one.

Maybe you grew up with an alcoholic. And now your children are growing up with an alcoholic you.

Perhaps you've been harassed sexually at work. Or maybe you're on the other end, the initiating end, of that sinister dynamic.

Villains and victims. Storm troopers and storm sufferers. Those who cause storms and those who must endure them. It was true for Isaiah in the 700's B.C., and it's true for people today in the twenty-first century. And when we think of these situations, it seems like they will always be at war. Assyrians and other villains will always stir up storms for other people; Israelites and other victims will always suffer storms of someone else's making. It seems like these opposing things will never meet, never find common ground, never be reconciled.

But then Isaiah envisions a dramatic shift in verses 6 and 7. Note how many times the word *all* appears in these two verses: "On this mountain, the LORD of heavenly forces will prepare for *all* peoples a rich feast, a feast of choice wines, of select foods rich in flavor, of choice wines well refined. He will swallow up on this mountain the veil that is veiling *all* peoples, the shroud enshrouding *all* nations" (italics added for emphasis). Isaiah paints a picture of all people coming together for a banquet, and *all* includes the Assyrians as well as the Israelites. The barrier vanishes. Villains and victims, Assyrians and Israelites, will at some point gather to have a great dinner together. Isaiah sees this vision of all peoples and all nations brought together by some miracle of God. At Good Shepherd, our mission statement is *inviting all people into a living relationship with Jesus Christ*. I have to tell you, we just love these verses!

REVERSAL, UPHEAVAL, AND SURPRISE WILL CHARACTERIZE OUR EXPERIENCE IN HEAVEN.

Yet I must ask you as you read verses 6 and 7: Are you OK with that? Are you all right with the possibility that God's love will conquer the death of murderers like Moses? of adulterers like David? of abusers like Amnon? Will it sit right with you if God's love is stronger than the death of today's terrorists? Can you accept it if God's love will overcome the death of those who kill in the name of Jesus, who doesn't believe in killing at all? Are you prepared for the unexpected to occur in the afterlife? Are you prepared to be surprised not only by who's *missing* from God's banquet but also by those who *made it* to the table? I am by no means a universalist, believing that everyone will ultimately be saved and live with God in heaven. But if Jesus' parables of the Kingdom tell us anything, they tell us that reversal, upheaval, and surprise will characterize our initial experience in heaven.

So how does this come about? When and where in the world will this happen, that Israelites and Assyrians, storm sufferers and storm causers, will gather like this? Look at Isaiah 25:8, where it all comes together:

> He will swallow up death forever. The LORD God will wipe tears from every face; he will remove his people's disgrace from off the whole earth, for the LORD has spoken.

God will swallow up death forever. That is a New Testament hope that forms the backbone of our Christian faith. In fact, Paul uses similar language, picking up on Isaiah's words almost verbatim in 1 Corinthians 15:54: "And when the rotting body has been clothed in what can't decay, and the dying body has been clothed in what can't die, then this statement in scripture will happen: *Death has been swallowed up by a victory.*" The promise that death will be swallowed up is an important New Testament truth, but Isaiah knew it long before Paul would pen his letter to Corinth.

Remember back in verse 1 when Isaiah mentioned God's wonderful things "planned long ago"? That placed him on God's eternal timeline, not his own calendar. We come back to that divine timeline now. And on God's eternal timeline, there is a coming day when death will be swallowed up. After death, on the other side of the grave, my death and your death and even death itself will be swallowed up in God's victory.

What's important to realize is that Isaiah's sense of shelter in 25:4 cannot be separated from the gift of assurance in 25:8. In other words, only when Isaiah remembers eternity, God's promise for the future, can he have any sense of peace or shelter in the present.

Today's peace comes from tomorrow's promise.

Because Isaiah knew what would happen when he died (his death would be swallowed by God's love), he could get through the storms while he lived. Because of his vision of God's eternal victory, he could deliver a message of praise in the middle of the Assyrian threat.

If you're in the middle of a storm that's not of your own making, a storm that shows no sign of letting up, here is what Isaiah says to you: ***The assurance of heaven is your shelter on earth.***

This is not a cliché; it's not a denial of how hard life can be; it's not a way of lip-synching your way through difficulty. It's a deeply God-centered way of looking at the world. This storm rages, but we know that it's temporary and short-lived when compared to the love for all eternity that awaits us. That truth, that assurance, that constant self-reminder, is not just a way of coping with our problems. It *is* shelter. It *is* peace. You have to anticipate Isaiah 25:8 to appreciate

THE ASSURANCE OF HEAVEN IS YOUR SHELTER ON EARTH.

Isaiah 25:4! *The assurance of heaven is your shelter on earth.*

You may have heard the line that "some people are so heavenly minded that they are no earthly good." As clever as that sounds, the reverse is true! The more heavenly minded you are, the more earthly serenity you receive, and the more good you can do.

Know this: If you trust in Christ for salvation (or even if you don't), you'll be dead a lot longer than you'll be alive. My mother is ninety-nine years old, and she still writes and plays tennis. That seems to us like a long time to remain active and healthy, but the fact is that ninety-nine years is still very short compared to eternity. The storm is temporary, but what happens after you die will last forever. And if you live in the confidence that Jesus Christ is victorious, that confidence will be your shelter in whatever storm may come. What death did to Jesus is nothing compared to what Jesus did to death. He swallowed death up in victory and rendered it powerless. That assurance can define your life. *The assurance of heaven is your shelter on earth.*

I remember from my days as a tournament tennis player that

the key to hitting a good shot was to see it before you *hit* it. The technique is called *visualization*, and it's especially effective with the serve. Many times before I'd line up to hit that shot, I'd see a perfect serve in my mind before I wound up to hit it. And with surprising regularity, it worked! It's a proven way of seeing where you're going before you even get there. As long as you don't lose sight of where you're going, you can make sense of today. You can handle the trip getting there. *The assurance—and anticipation—of heaven is your shelter on earth.*

One lady on the American frontier, before she died, told her family that she wanted to be buried to the east of their cabin, with her feet pointed to the east. Why? "So that when I get up on resurrection morn the sun will be in my face!" When you have that kind of trust and confidence and even anticipation, you can endure anything. *The assurance of heaven is your shelter on earth.*

Once eternity is settled, everything else in life comes into proper perspective. One of Methodism's many gifts to the larger world of Christian thought is our doctrine of *assurance*. It's the first cousin of what our Baptist friends call "once saved, always saved" and what our Presbyterian siblings call "the perseverance of the saints." Methodism's teaching on assurance reminds us that while it's possible for a person of faith later to deny that faith (see Hebrews 6:4-8, for example), such denial is by no means inevitable. Why? Because God's Spirit confirms with our spirit that we have been bought by Jesus' blood and filled with his Spirit, and our place in God's eternity is secured. We can *know* that when death comes, we will live and reign in Christ's presence forever. Fanny Crosby, who wrote the hymn "Blessed Assurance," wasn't a Methodist...but she should have been! *The assurance of heaven is your shelter on earth.*

It's not a cliché; it's a gift from God. When I was a teenager, very early in my Christian journey, I still struggled with acne. This may seem trifling now, but when you're a teenager and you wake up with a new blemish, believe me, that's a storm! I wanted God to take it away, and I even prayed for it. But it didn't work out that way. And yet somehow I didn't get bitter that God didn't miraculously take my acne away. I learned to say to myself, *This is temporary, and a pimple-free heaven will be forever!* It seems small now, but at the time it wasn't. The knowledge of my eternity really did give me comfort during that storm of my teenage years. *The assurance of heaven is your shelter on earth.*

The assurance of heaven is a shelter not just during small storms like acne but during life's worst hurricanes as well. That is exactly what Isaiah faced in the Assyrian army that threatened Jerusalem. The Assyrian storm threatened the prophet's life and the lives of everyone he knew. The people of Judah had no doubt heard what atrocities the Assyrians committed against the people of conquered cities. But for Isaiah, the knowledge that death itself would be swallowed up allowed him to proclaim God as "a hiding place from the storm" (Isaiah 25:4).

IN THE END, THE VILLAINS COME TO THE BANQUET TOO.

This knowledge and comfort encompasses more than just Isaiah and his people. God will provide a banquet of rich, fine food for "all peoples," including the ruthless Assyrians who are causing Isaiah's storms. The villains come to the banquet too. Make no mistake: God brings about destruction and calamity to humble the strong and arrogant, turning their fortified towns and fortresses into ruins so that they will glorify and fear God (Isaiah 25:2-3). But in the end, the villains come to the banquet too. And this is good news.

Why is this good news? Because you might be the one causing the very storms that make your loved ones suffer. You might be the villain, not the victim—the strong-armed storm causer of Isaiah 25. Maybe someone else is hoping that God will send calamity your way to ensure your humility and to make a storm stop. And I don't know about you, but for me it's good news that God has a future for the villains and the storm causers too. It's good news that death will be swallowed up for all, that God is preparing a banquet for all. Maybe you're living for now, for today, and God wants to reorient your perspective so that you too will be living on God's time, with an eye on eternity.

God longs for life for all. God doesn't desire that death be swallowed up for some—the chosen or church people—but for all. Your current path as a villain or storm causer is a path to death, and God doesn't want that. There will be an empty seat at the banquet table if you're not there.

And the best news of all to me is this: Every bit of shelter you get now is a down payment on the eternal, indestructible shelter of eternity. Shelter can take various forms to offer you comfort: a prayer, someone's help, a meal, a card, an unexpected feeling of comfort. During any of those moments when you feel dry in the downpour, you receive a glimpse of the fullness of your eternity with God.

I had an experience of this not too long ago. It was a Friday, my usual day off, and I got a voicemail. Now, that particular week had been full of frustration that our church wasn't growing as quickly as I thought it should have been. In the all-pervasive "who's got the biggest church?" competition, I kept falling short. So with a little bit of dread, I listened to the voicemail, fearing more bad news. But instead of more despair, I listened as a friend's voice on the other end said, "I know Friday is your day off, so I almost didn't call you, but then I decided I would. I just wanted you to know that your words on Sundays have brought me to life. I'm so glad that you're not only my preacher but also my friend." Whoa! I'll take that on a day off! As I finished listening, I realized that this little bit of shelter, as marvelous as it was, is just a hint, just a shadow, of unending, everlasting shelter and love and affirmation in the life to come. Because I anticipate *that,* I can endure *this.*

There's something I get to say at a lot of funerals, especially when I know the person had a living relationship with Jesus Christ: "She is more alive right now than she's ever been before."

That's not a trite expression; it's a bedrock truth of the universe. When you die in Christ, you are more alive than you have ever been before. When that truth soaks into who you are and what you are about, you can endure any storm. When you know what's coming, you receive shelter in the midst of this life's tempests.

If you're going through a storm right now, remind yourself of this daily...hourly if you need to. *The assurance of heaven is your shelter on earth.*

Questions for Reflection and Discussion

Write responses and other thoughts in the space below each question. If you are discussing the book in a small group, prepare for the meeting by writing answers in advance.

1. Think of storms that have arisen throughout your life. What are some shelters you sought that *didn't* work? What do those failed shelters have in common?

2. What, if any, are some shelters that have proven more enduring and effective?

3. Name someone who goes through stormy seasons with unusual calm. To what do you attribute that person's serenity?

4. In 1 Corinthians 15:54, Paul quotes and reapplies Isaiah 25:8. What does that tell you about Paul's understanding of the Hebrew Scriptures?

5. How does this connection help you see the Scriptures differently?

6. How do you draw comfort from your confidence and assurance in Christ?

7. Look up the following Scripture passages: 2 Corinthians 4:1-18; Philippians 1:1-29; and Romans 8:18. How do these verses put your present difficulties in perspective?

8. What other Scripture passages do you turn to in order to gain God's perspective on your life?

9. What are some storms affecting your community right now? What about our country or our world as a whole?

10. How can our assurance of God's victory provide shelter from these storms? What hope do they offer? How can you communicate this hope to the people around you?

Assure Your Neighbor

Write the words of Romans 8:18 on a card: *I believe that the present suffering is nothing compared to the coming glory that is going to be revealed to us.*

Now…who in your life needs to hear that truth this week? Once you determine who, give that person the Romans 8:18 card you have made. Pray that it will be help assure them and be a shelter for them.

Closing Prayer

Father, thank you for your assurance. We praise you that our salvation does not depend on our performance for you but our position in you. And please receive all the glory for the ways in which the assurance of tomorrow helps today make more sense. Amen.

Daily Scripture Readings

This week, read the following Scripture passages. Rest in the assurance God gives you each day.

Monday: 1 Corinthians 15:1-34
Tuesday: 1 Corinthians 15:35-58
Wednesday: 2 Corinthians 4:1-18
Thursday: Philippians 1:1-29
Friday: Matthew 6:25-34; Romans 8:18

1. From *The NIV Application Commentary: Jonah, Nahum, Habakkuk, Zephaniah,* by James K. Bruckner (Zondervan, 2004); page 28.

4

THE PERFECT STORM

Last night an angel from the God to whom I belong and whom I worship stood beside me. (Acts 27:23)

Luke is a genius.

By Luke, I mean the guy who wrote the Gospel of Luke, the third in the quartet of New Testament writings we often let slip off our tongues as one long whole: *MatthewMarkLukeandJohn.*

Each of these Gospel writers communicates something profound about Jesus' life and identity. But Luke—physician, journalist, adventurer, and note-taker *extraordinaire*—is a bona fide literary genius.

I want to hammer that idea home because in studying Scripture, we often make the mistake of looking at *what* the words say without exploring *how* they say it. We come to the Bible for its theological meaning without appreciating its artistic skill. And the fact is that the authors of the biblical library are not only without peer in their understanding of God; they are also thoughtful practitioners of the craft of writing . . . none more so than Dr. Luke, who—say it with me now—is a *genius.*

We see his genius especially in all the subtle asides, what we might call "the land between the commas." Throughout his work, we can find comments that seem almost like throwaways, things that appear insignificant at first. But when you look more closely at them, you find that they are actually loaded with meaning.

That characteristic is true not only for the Gospel of Luke but also for the Book of Acts, which the same author wrote as a companion piece, or sequel. For Luke, the story doesn't end with the death and resurrection of Jesus; it continues through the spread of the gospel by Jesus' earliest followers. If the Gospel of Luke is a biography of Jesus, the Book of Acts is like the biography of the Holy Spirit as told through the growth and adventures of the church in the first thirty years or so after Jesus died and rose again.

THE PERFECT STORM

In most places, Acts reads like an adventure novel, with the bustling movement of the Holy Spirit, the rapid spread of the gospel, and unexpected plot twists along the way. Toward the end, it takes on the characteristics of *Robinson Crusoe*. Paul is a former persecutor of the church who has a vision of Christ and becomes one of Jesus' most devoted followers (plot twist!). In the last several chapters of Acts, Paul is a prisoner, and his crime is being a public Christian. He has appealed to Rome, even to Caesar himself, and by some vagaries of Roman law, his appeal must be heard. So the Romans put Paul and a number of other prisoners onto a cargo ship loaded down with grain as it heads from what is today Israel to the boot of Italy.

While out on the Mediterranean, they run into a perfect storm. As you read through this storm story, pay attention to the details.

Luke, literary genius that he is, embeds some deep meaning within them. Here is the story of Paul's storm in Acts 27:13-44:

> When a gentle south wind began to blow, they thought they could carry out their plan. They pulled up anchor and sailed closely along the coast of Crete. Before long, a hurricane-strength wind known as a northeaster swept down from Crete.
>
> The ship was caught in the storm and couldn't be turned into the wind. So we gave in to it, and it carried us along. After sailing under the shelter of an island called Cauda, we were able to control the lifeboat only with difficulty. They brought the lifeboat aboard, then began to wrap the ship with cables to hold it together. Fearing they might run aground on the sandbars of the Gulf of Syrtis, they lowered the anchor and let the ship be carried along. We were so battered by the violent storm that the next day the men began throwing cargo overboard. On the third day, they picked up the ship's gear and hurled it into the sea. When neither the sun nor the moon appeared for many days and the raging storm continued to pound us, all hope of our being saved from this peril faded.
>
> For a long time no one had eaten. Paul stood up among them and said, "Men, you should have complied with my instructions not to sail from Crete. Then we would have avoided this damage and loss. Now I urge you to be encouraged. Not one of your lives will be lost, though we will lose the ship. Last night an angel from the God to whom I belong and whom I worship stood beside me. The angel said, 'Don't be afraid, Paul! You must stand before Caesar! Indeed, God has also graciously given you everyone

sailing with you.' Be encouraged, men! I have faith in God that it will be exactly as he told me. However, we must run aground on some island."

On the fourteenth night, we were being carried across the Adriatic Sea. Around midnight the sailors began to suspect that land was near. They dropped a weighted line to take soundings and found the water to be about one hundred twenty feet deep. After proceeding a little farther, we took soundings again and found the water to be about ninety feet deep. Afraid that we might run aground somewhere on the rocks, they hurled out four anchors from the stern and began to pray for daylight. The sailors tried to abandon the ship by lowering the lifeboat into the sea, pretending they were going to lower anchors from the bow. [31] Paul said to the centurion and his soldiers, "Unless they stay in the ship, you can't be saved from peril." The soldiers then cut the ropes to the lifeboat and let it drift away.

Just before daybreak, Paul urged everyone to eat. He said, "This is the fourteenth day you've lived in suspense, and you've not had even a bite to eat. I urge you to take some food. Your health depends on it. None of you will lose a single hair from his head." After he said these things, he took bread, gave thanks to God in front of them all, then broke it and began to eat. Everyone was encouraged and took some food. (In all, there were two hundred seventy-six of us on the ship.) When they had eaten as much as they wanted, they lightened the ship by throwing the grain into the sea.

In the morning light they saw a bay with a sandy beach. They didn't know what land it was, but they thought they might possibly be able to run the ship aground. They cut the anchors loose and left them in the sea. At the same time, they untied the ropes that ran back to the rudders. They raised the foresail to catch the wind and made for the beach. But they struck a sandbar and the ship ran aground. The bow was stuck and wouldn't move, and the stern was broken into pieces by the force of the waves. The soldiers decided to kill the prisoners to keep them from swimming to shore and escaping. However, the centurion wanted to save Paul, so he stopped them from carrying out their plan. He ordered those who could swim to jump overboard first and head for land. He ordered the rest to grab hold of planks or debris from the ship. In this way, everyone reached land safely.

I call this the perfect storm. Why do I say that? Look at verse 27, about midway through this long story:

> On the fourteenth night, we were being carried across the Adriatic Sea. Around midnight the sailors began to suspect that land was near.

They were still on the sea after the *fourteenth night* of the storm! I told you above that Luke can pack a lot into a single phrase that we might not give much thought. We read along in verses 13-26, and we see that they're sort of in a tough situation. But all of a sudden, in one little comment, Luke makes it clear that this is no ordinary storm. Things are much worse than we readers have realized. Two weeks is a monster storm! That is two weeks of seasickness, two weeks of harrowing escapes, two weeks of rain-soaked danger, and two weeks of close contact with no plumbing or bathing. It's a perfect storm because it seems like a never-ending storm.

There are perfect storms in life that just keep going and going, aren't there? There are things like a health crisis you're in the middle of, and just when you get a sliver of good news, some bad news follows. And if the crisis involves mental health rather than physical health, the issues can be that much more unpredictable and that much more enduring.

Other perfect storms might involve an adult son or daughter who keeps returning home and can't seem to make his or her own way in the world. Parents and children alike experience that situation as a storm, each in their own way. Or the storm might be financial troubles or struggles in one's job or career. The more you work on them, the worse they seem to get. Or it might be something else entirely. But whatever it is, a perfect storm, a never-ending storm, rages around you and sweeps you off course, threatening to wash you under. We all know what it's like to be tossed about in a storm, and then, all of a sudden, we look down and realize we're in the fourteenth day of a perfect(ly) long storm. Some of us are experiencing that at this very moment.

Given our familiarity with life's storms, it's important for us to notice how this perfect storm starts. Look at the beginning of it in Acts 27:13:

> When a gentle south wind began to blow, they thought they could carry out their plan.

I love that: "They thought they could carry out their plan." A gentle south breeze began to blow, and they thought they had just what they wanted. But that dream wind quickly became a nightmare storm. It's kind of like that old saying "Be careful what you wish for; you just might get it!" Sometimes we want our plans to work out, not realizing that if they do, we'll get a bit more than we have bargained for. Our successes often come back to haunt us:

"Oh, he's cute!"

"Man, she's gorgeous!"

"Here's the house!"

"This is the last job I'll ever need!"

And my favorite: "Finally! I found a church that meets my needs!"

And then, sure enough, those people or situations turn on you. It's not that you wanted too much; it's that you wanted the wrong thing. You have your plan all figured out, and everything seems to be falling into place. But then that situation of "just what you wanted" quickly turns into a perfect storm of trouble. The new romance turns out to be a soul-quenching, purity-stealing dead-end relationship. The perfect house comes with those abominable neighbors. That ideal job was available in the first place because the boss had run the previous three employees off. And the local church that fit like a glove turns out to have more than a few holes in it. The gentle, welcome breeze sometimes becomes a squall that catches you up and drives you off course. And that's exactly what happens on Paul's ship. In verse 14 we read:

> Before long, a hurricane-strength wind known as a northeaster swept down from Crete.

IT'S NOT THAT YOU WANTED TOO MUCH; IT'S THAT YOU WANTED THE WRONG THING.

That gentle south wind drew them out onto the water and made them vulnerable to a nor'easter. Whether it's the Mediterranean Sea in the first century or the Atlantic today, nor'easters are bad news! They had tried to sail in relative safety along the coast of Crete (verse 13), but the wind pushed them away from the island and across the Mediterranean, toward modern-day Libya. This leads to days of being tossed, turned, beaten, and battered by the wind and the waves.

Luke experienced this nor'easter and the ensuing storm first-hand because he was on the ship. We know that from 27:15 and other verses, where the author writes that "we gave in to it, and it carried us along." Not *they*. *We*. Luke was one of the people on the ship living through the storm. And Luke, the literary genius, shows us an interesting pattern of how the sailors and the others dealt with the storm. We can see the pattern by looking at verses 18, 19, 32, 38, and 42-44:

> We were so battered by the violent storm that the next day the men began throwing cargo overboard. (27:18)

Cargo goes overboard...

> On the third day, they picked up the ship's gear and hurled it into the sea. (27:19)

Tackle goes overboard...

> The soldiers then cut the ropes to the lifeboat and let it drift away. (27:32)

Lifeboat is cut loose...

> When they had eaten as much as they wanted, they lightened the ship by throwing the grain into the sea. (27:38)

Grain goes overboard...

> The soldiers decided to kill the prisoners to keep them from swimming to shore and escaping. However, the

centurion wanted to save Paul, so he stopped them from carrying out their plan. He ordered those who could swim to jump overboard first and head for land. He ordered the rest to grab hold of planks or debris from the ship. In this way, everyone reached land safely. (27:42-44)

Even people go overboard!

In the pattern Luke sets up, which probably follows the actual practice on board, the boat keeps getting lighter. See, the heavier a ship is in a storm, the more vulnerable it is to the wind and the waves. When the seas are rough and the storm is heavy, the ship has to be buoyant to survive. So Luke tells us—because Luke was probably doing it—that the sailors, soldiers, and prisoners grabbed the trunks, barrels, boxes, whatever else they could find, and heaved all the unnecessary things over the side of the ship and into the sea. Even the things that were necessary under normal conditions, like the ship's gear, the food, and the lifeboat, had to be jettisoned during the storm.

The pattern is unmistakable: To survive the perfect storm, you've got to lighten the load. You've got to have less stuff. It hurt like the devil every time they had to lift and throw, but their survival depended on it. And notice the escalating importance: cargo, navigation, transportation, and then even the food.

And then in the middle of all that, Paul gives a line that shines God's perspective on throwing all these things overboard. Earlier Paul had given some advice that attempting to travel at this time of year would be dangerous (27:9-10). If the soldiers and sailors had listened to him, they would have avoided the storm altogether. But now Paul passes on a message of God, which encourages and reassures the others on board that their lives will be saved:

> Last night an angel from the God to whom I belong and whom I worship stood beside me. The angel said,

> "Don't be afraid, Paul! You must stand before Caesar!
> Indeed, God has also graciously given you everyone
> sailing with you." Be encouraged, men! I have faith in
> God that it will be exactly as he told me. (27:23-25)

Paul received assurance that his life would be spared as well as
the lives of the others on his ship. Not even the perfect storm can
stand up to God's purpose for Paul, that he testify about Christ
before Caesar. But what I am more interested in is the way Paul
describes his relationship with God: "the God to whom I belong
and whom I worship" (verse 23). *The God to whom I belong.* In
other words, Paul doesn't *have* all those possessions like cargo or
gear; he is the possession! He can be part of throwing all that stuff
overboard in a storm because he is owned by God more than he
owns anything.

I get the sense here that in this one line, nestled in the land
between the commas, is the purpose of the storm. God sends the
storm and then allows its epic duration so that Paul and Luke
and the others will discover that *being the possession* is far more
important than *having possessions.* And if God has to empty an
entire ship of its cargo to prove a point, then God will do it.

Do you know what Luke is telling us ... especially those of us
caught in a perfect, unending storm? **The longer the storm, the
lighter you travel.**

God can still the storm; we saw that in Mark 4:35-41. But
sometimes God allows the storm to go on because there's some
area, some habit, some relationship, some *thing,* that's weighing you
down. And God wants you to do the arduous lifting of throwing it
overboard. God wants you to know: *The longer the storm, the lighter
you travel.*

Maybe it's like those two guys who went deer hunting one
time. A few hours later, one of them emerged from the woods and
headed toward his friends, carrying this enormous eight-point buck
with him. His buddies said to him, "Great deer, but where's Harry?
He went into the woods with you!"

"Oh," the man answered, "he fainted about a mile back in the woods from helping me carry the buck."

His friends were surprised. "You mean you left him lying there alone and carried the deer back?"

The man replied, "It was a tough call, but I figured of the two, no one is going to come along and steal Harry." *The longer the storm, the lighter you travel.*

Or it's like the pastor friend I know who became a much sought-after speaker on the Christian conference circuit after a season of unprecedented growth in the congregation he serves. And yet after a couple of years of saying yes to all those invitations, he had a penetrating realization: He was spending more time talking about his church than serving in it. And so, for the sake of that congregation's health and his own sanity, he began throwing those speaking engagement invitations overboard. His true calling is to serve in his church, not talk about it. *The longer the storm, the lighter you travel.*

Many of us struggle to manage our priorities, maintaining a healthy balance between family, work, and faith. One man I know

THE LONGER THE STORM, THE LIGHTER YOU TRAVEL.

decided to think of it this way: "Who will be crying at your funeral? That's where you invest the time." In other words, you prioritize the people who are most important, so when it's time to travel lightly in the storm, you know what you can afford to throw overboard. *The longer the storm, the lighter you travel.*

Let me ask you: What do you need to throw overboard? Where and how do you need to lighten the load in your life during the storms you experience? What is it that you hang on to for dear life but in reality is unnecessary?

WHAT DO YOU NEED TO THROW OVERBOARD?

For some of you, it's that relationship. It could be a romantic relationship, maybe even headed to the altar, but it's already toxic. Deep down you recognize that you've already compromised much of what you believe for the sake of that relationship. Or maybe it's not even a romantic relationship—a group of friends or coworkers, for instance—but it has that same net effect. There is a toxin there that keeps you in storm-fighting mode and compromises some of your most deeply held convictions. *The longer the storm, the lighter you travel.*

For others, that excess cargo can be quite different. Maybe it's your sense of image; you spend so much time perfecting and protecting your reputation and how others see you, eventually it feels like there's no "you" anymore at all. If I'm being honest, I have to admit this is my tendency. Take that concern with image, combine it with a strong desire to be right, and you've got cargo that weighs me down in the storm. God is working on me to show me I already have God's affirmation, so I can be wrong on some things and the world will still turn. Cast it overboard. *The longer the storm, the lighter you travel.*

Maybe it's a habit that God desperately wants you to throw into the sea so you can survive. It could be smoking...of the legal variety—or smoking...of the illegal variety! If it's one of those kinds of habits, please let me say a word to my younger readers: Throw it overboard now. The longer it remains embedded in your life, the harder it will be to stop. Think about it this way: What's easier to pull out of the ground—a small sapling or a whole tree? In the same way, when a habit becomes deeply rooted inside you for years and years, it's that much harder to uproot and throw out. And you must throw it out in order to survive. *The longer the storm, the lighter you travel.*

Have you ever noticed that the more you have, the more time and money you spend caring for it? Around Charlotte, where I live, I have observed that storage units are a significant growth industry. I see them everywhere. I suspect it's the same for many other cities. Even during the worst parts of our recent recession, companies providing storage units have done well. Why do we have storage units? Because we have too much stuff! I've been speaking about metaphorical cargo, like addictions or toxic relationships, but it's true for physical possessions too. We possess too many things, and we have to spend extra money just to keep it all locked up somewhere. Where has stuff or its pursuit made you vulnerable in the storm? Where is it that God is prolonging the storm so that you will sell, give, or trash all in order that you might fully tithe? *The longer the storm, the lighter you travel.*

This is true even of the seemingly good things in our lives. A lot of church folk resist change, reluctant to give up their hold on what the church is. But what so many don't realize is, they are holding on to what church *used to be.* Their sense of religion has glorified the past so much that the future has dried up. It can even be true of Good Shepherd, where I serve, though we strive to do new things in reaching new people for Christ. I got the greatest e-mail awhile back from someone who had recently been wrestling with this very issue:

> Talbot, it was so good to be at Good Shepherd yesterday after all this time away. We realized we were longing for a church that no longer exists. We also realized that when you resist change in a church you are often resisting the move of the Holy Spirit.

When I read that, I saw someone tossing unnecessary cargo overboard. *The longer the storm, the lighter you travel.*

The men onboard Paul's ship had to lighten the load in order to survive their storm. But there's another terrific detail in this story, which teaches something else about surviving life's storms. In Acts 27:20, Luke writes the following:

> When neither the sun nor the moon appeared for many days and the raging storm continued to pound us, all hope of our being saved from this peril faded.

During the worst part of the storm, the people on the boat went many days without seeing the sun or the moon. Do you know what that means? They had no guidance, no heavenly bodies to help them navigate. If you couldn't see the stars in those days, you were sailing blind. There was no real way to tell where they were or where they were headed, much less any means of controlling their course. And as bad as the storm was, it was this situation—the loss of navigation—that caused them to despair of being rescued. If there's no guidance, things can become hopeless.

How many of us navigate storms with no guidance? Prayer, the Scriptures, a small group, a support group, a therapist, or some other support system offers us a valuable means of guidance to navigate life's storms. Without these things, you're all alone in rough seas. And maybe an attitude of self-reliance keeps you from seeking these things out; maybe you have convinced yourself that, sun and moon or not, you can find your way alone. That attitude becomes your cargo, and it weighs you down. Toss that mindset overboard and get serious about the guidance you need!

There is, of course, the other extreme. Some people are *too* reliant on guides, dragging too many people into their lives. They have a way of spreading their storms to others. You know what I'm saying because I alluded to it in Chapter 2: They're storm chasers. In that storm chasing (and, if we're honest, also a bit of storm creating), they've become experts at being helpless. They insist that others within their orbit embrace their problem as forcefully as they do. And they become highly indignant whenever others don't cooperate with their codependent plans. If that's you, then toss that mindset overboard too. *The longer the storm, the lighter you travel.*

SOMETIMES ALL YOU HAVE LEFT IS THE ONE WHO HAS YOU.

Sometimes it can feel as if you are hit by the perfect storm. Not every storm is like this; in fact, most are not. But sometimes the storm takes away everything you hold dear. You get rid of the cargo, the tackle, even the lifeboat and the food. And the storm keeps raging. But look at how the story ends:

> However, the centurion wanted to save Paul, so he stopped them from carrying out their plan. He ordered those who could swim to jump overboard first and head for land. He ordered the rest to grab hold of planks or debris from the ship. In this way, everyone reached land safely. (Acts 27:43-44)

They lose the ship itself. The storm takes away everything but their lives. But God is with them, because remember what Paul has already told us in verse 23: "Last night an angel from the God to whom I belong and whom I worship stood beside me." And that is more than enough. Paul has fewer possessions, but because he belongs to God, he can endure the storm with confidence.

There may come a time when you have nothing left but the debris of your life . . . and the one who has you. In those moments, if they come, remember that you belong to God. Is God taking you there? Are you enduring a storm, which might just bring you to the place where it's all gone but the one who remains? Is God taking you to a place where you have nothing left, which means you have everything you need? *The longer the storm, the lighter you travel.*

Questions for Reflection and Discussion

Write responses and other thoughts in the space below each question. If you are discussing the book in a small group, prepare for the meeting by writing answers in advance.

1. What's the longest storm you've personally endured? How open were you to teachable moments within that storm?

2. How much cargo is on your ship? Consider your habits and relationships as well as your material possessions.

3. Have you ever tossed something overboard in your life, realizing later that you never needed it in the first place? What was that experience like? How might it empower you to do it again?

4. Look up Philippians 3:7-14, which is one of the daily Scripture readings for this week. Read this passage out loud, in a group if possible. Would you say Paul wrote those words before or after his experience on the ship in Acts 27? How do the words of that letter influence your interpretation of Paul's storm experience?

5. As you think about the church and religious life in America, what unnecessary cargo do you find in your own attitudes toward the church? Do you experience nostalgia? negative feelings? How might this cargo be holding you back? How is God calling you to let go of it?

6. What will you discard this week to travel lighter?

7. In what way do you consider yourself someone who is possessed by God? How does belonging to God change your way of thinking about your own possessions?

Praise the One Who Has You

Listen to the song "One Thing Remains," by Jesus Culture. A video for the song can be accessed on YouTube at the following link: *https://www.youtube.com/watch?v=6_KXsMCJgBQ*

As you view or listen, pay attention to how the lyrics praise Christ for being all-sufficient, with a love and grace that go on and on. If you are studying THE STORM BEFORE THE CALM in a group, bring your session to a close by listening to this glorious declaration of the sufficiency of Christ.

Closing Prayer

Lord Jesus, thank you for Luke's genius! Praise you for the land between the commas. And most of all, thank you that I am your possession. Enable me to travel light this week. Amen.

Daily Scripture Readings

This week, read the following Scripture passages. Ask how God is calling you to travel more lightly.

Monday: Acts 27:1-12
Tuesday: Acts 27:13-44
Wednesday: Acts 28:1-10
Thursday: Acts 28:11-31
Friday: Philippians 3:7-14

5

AFTER THE STORM

Noah, a farmer, made a new start and planted a vineyard.
(Genesis 9:20)

Most of us know the biblical story of Noah and the Flood. Even if you didn't learn about it in church or Sunday school growing up, you've probably heard about it at some point just because it's a familiar part of our culture. There was even a movie based on the story in 2014, starring Russell Crowe. The basic narrative goes like this: God sees humankind's evil and violence and determines to destroy all life with a great flood. But Noah, a righteous man, finds favor with God, and God decides to spare Noah and his family. God instructs Noah to build an ark, or large boat, and bring a male and female of every kind of animal onboard along with his wife, his three sons, and their wives. It rains for forty days and forty nights, drowning every living thing on earth, but those onboard the ark are saved. When the Flood subsides, the survivors exit the ark and repopulate the earth. God makes an agreement with Noah never again to destroy all life with a flood and makes the rainbow as a sign of this covenant.

The Flood story has more details and some interesting subthemes, but that's the basic narrative we've all learned. But what you may not know is this: The story of Noah and his family doesn't end there. There's a short episode that occurs after they exit the ark that casts Noah and his family in some less-than-ideal light. Our discussion of Scripture's storm stories would be incomplete without considering this story of what happens after the storm. And it has much to teach us. We find it in Genesis 9:18-27:

> Noah's sons Shem, Ham, and Japheth came out of the ark. Now Ham was Canaan's father. These were Noah's three sons, and from them the whole earth was populated. Noah, a farmer, made a new start and planted a vineyard. He drank some of the wine, became drunk, and took off his clothes in his tent. Ham, Canaan's father, saw his father naked and told his two brothers who were outside. Shem and Japheth took a robe, threw it over their shoulders, walked backward, and covered their naked father without looking at him because they turned away. When Noah woke up from his wine, he discovered what his youngest son had done to him. He said,
>
> > "Cursed be Canaan:
> > the lowest servant
> > he will be for his brothers."
>
> He also said,
>
> > "Bless the LORD,
> > the God of Shem;
> > Canaan will be his servant.
> > May God give space to Japheth;
> > he will live in Shem's tents,
> > and Canaan will be his servant."

Well, *that* part sure didn't make it into your illustrated children's Bibles, did it?

In the afterglow of surviving the destruction of the rest of the known world, in the euphoria of making it through the storm to end all storms (the likes of which we'll never see again!), Noah plants a vineyard. He reaps the harvest, stomps the grapes, ferments the juice, and decides to sample some of his own product. All right, he samples a *lot* of his own product! And he ends up getting stone-cold drunk, passing out naked in his own tent. I don't know about you, but I don't see that picture in the children's Bible I got for my kids.

THERE IS MORE DANGER AFTER SUCCESS THAN AFTER FAILURE.

But Genesis doesn't omit that part of the story. It narrates Noah's flaws as well as his righteousness because the ancestors of our faith were real, imperfect people like you and me. And there are things we can learn from their faults, just as we can learn from their successes. So what does this piece of the story from after the storm tell us? That if you were cooped up on a boat with a bunch of animals for a year, you'd drink too much too?

No. It tells us that we have the most vulnerability after we've had the greatest accomplishment. There is more danger after success than after failure. When you've had success upon success and you're at the top, there's nowhere to go but down. And when we reach that peak, that's when we're the most vulnerable.

It's why repeat champions are so rare in sports.

It's why entertainers are on the top of the charts one week and in rehab the next.

It's why the pastors on the highest pedestals have the steepest falls.

It's why some of you treat yourself after that great sale or that great project with just a little too much to drink or a little too much attention from the opposite sex.

It's a similar trap that Noah falls into, giving in to a careless kind of euphoria. He ends up in a drunken, naked stupor, which hardly befits his identity as head of the only family on earth worth saving from the Flood. But Noah's actions result in more than just personal embarrassment. They open a rift in his family that will last for generations, the effects of which we still feel today. While Noah is passed out, his son Ham "saw his father naked and told his two brothers who were outside" (Genesis 9:22). Noah's drunken stupor involves the whole family in a scandal, which will quickly take a turn for the worst.

Now, to us, what Ham witnesses is no big deal. Lots of boys have seen their dads in the bathroom at home or the locker room at the gym. It can be awkward or embarrassing, but it's nothing worth losing sleep over.

But in Noah's day and in the days of the Scripture writers, for reasons that are not entirely clear to us, it *was* a big deal. Some experts have suggested that there was more involved in this incident than merely seeing, as if sight were a metaphor for something worse, like incest or abuse. Others have said that Noah's nakedness really means his wife's nakedness, so that Ham saw her inappropriately or even witnessed an act of intimacy between his mom and dad. In some of the laws in Leviticus, "uncovering someone's nakedness" means having sexual relations with them, and there's a close link between one's father's nakedness and his wife's nakedness. So these conjectures about what exactly Ham did are well founded. But for reasons I will mention, in this case I think that seeing is what it actually means. The offense is in what Ham saw, namely his father's nakedness. In doing so, he violated his father's dignity. And to make matters worse, he went out and told his two brothers about it, doubling the disrespect and multiplying the violation.

Maybe you know something of what this is like. Maybe you have been disrespected or betrayed in some way by the people closest to you. Maybe, like Noah, you thought you could trust certain people only to find out that your trust was misplaced. Or perhaps you're on the other side of the situation, playing the role of Ham. You're the one betraying someone else's trust, disrespecting someone you should honor and love.

One man's careless elation and another's disrespectful violation sets in motion a chain of events of inevitable pain and messiness. The Flood was terrible, but as it turns out, life after the storm is sometimes not much better.

NOAH AND ADAM

If you read Noah's story carefully, you'll notice some significant parallels between Noah and Adam, the first human (see Genesis 2–3). Both men are the ancestors of all human life, since Adam was the first human and Noah is the progenitor of everyone who survived the Flood. Both men experience a fall involving fruit, with Adam eating the forbidden fruit (Genesis 3:1-24) and Noah getting drunk from wine. And both men experience shame involving nakedness, as Adam realizes his nakedness (Genesis 3:7) and Noah's nakedness is on display for his son to see.

These details show us that Genesis is a brilliant work of art. But more than that, they show us something important about human nature. Time may be linear, but human behavior is cyclical.

We keep making the same messes over and over and over again. And in the case of both Noah and Adam, their mistakes create a mess for their descendants, who have to deal with the fallout of their actions.

...which brings up Shem and Japheth, Noah's other two sons. Ham tells them about what he has seen inside Noah's tent. Look at what they do when they hear about it:

> Shem and Japheth took a robe, threw it over their shoulders, walked backward, and covered their naked father without looking at him because they turned away. (Genesis 9:23)

The scene unfolds in such detail. They place the garment on their shoulders, do the world's first moonwalk, and in an act of utmost respect, lay the garment over their naked, drunk father. By walking backward, they keep their faces turned the other way so that they won't see Noah in this condition. I mentioned above that I think Ham's offense was visual—that when it says he "saw" his father, it simply means that he actually saw him and nothing more. That's because his brothers go to extraordinary lengths to avoid seeing their father and thereby avoid the offense that Ham committed. Shem and Japheth take great care to rectify the situation without making things worse.

It's important to realize that Shem and Japheth take these first tentative, delicate steps toward making right the situation that Noah's and Ham's actions have brought about. Life often works that way, doesn't it? One or two people make the mess, and it's up to someone else to start cleaning it up.

Unfortunately, Shem and Japheth are unable to fix things entirely. They avoid seeing their father naked, and they successfully cover him up to prevent further damage to his dignity. But that dignity has already suffered a violation through Ham, who not only saw his father naked but also went and told his brothers about it. That offense cannot be undone, and it has consequences. When

Noah wakes up—I love that phrasing, "woke up from his wine"—he discovers what has happened to him (9:24). He utters a curse upon Canaan, Ham's son, as a way of punishing Ham for what he has done:

> "Cursed be Canaan:
>   the lowest servant
>   he will be for his brothers."

He also said,

> "Bless the LORD,
>   the God of Shem;
> Canaan will be his servant.
> May God give space to Japheth;
>   he will live in Shem's tents,
>   and Canaan will be his servant."

In the past, these words have erroneously been used to justify the American slave trade and racism, with people applying this curse to Africans and African Americans, saying they are the descendants of Canaan. But nothing could be further from the truth. The curse envisions the ancient Canaanites, the closest enemies of the Israelite people. The Canaanites were a significant threat to the Israelites, and this curse in part explained the Israelites' ability to conquer them. And pay close attention to the source of the curse; it comes not from God, but from Noah. And Noah is likely hung over when he utters it! So this curse is not some divine decree that places one race of people below another. It's the utterance of a flawed human being, which has lasting consequences in Israel's own time period. To read it as a justification for slavery or racism is an absurd, wrongful abuse of the text. It shows that the Bible can be dangerous in the wrong hands.

Now that we have established what Noah's curse does *not* mean, we can turn our attention to what it *does* mean. As I said, it envisions the ancient Canaanite people, who were some of Israel's closest enemies. It supported the Israelite view that the land of Canaan, which God would promise to give to Abraham and his descendants, was the rightful possession of the Israelite people. It supported the Israelite view that the people who lived there, the Canaanites, were evil and that it was God's plan for the Israelites to conquer them and enslave them. And this viewpoint, of course, has lent itself to war and conflict in the ancient world that reappears even today between Israel and its neighbors in the Middle East. This incident in the tent after the storm sets in motion an ongoing rivalry between kinsfolk in Genesis and unrelenting strife in that part of the world today. One man's careless euphoria and another man's calculated disrespect create a mess than endures for generations. It's a never-ending debris field. Shem and Japheth started the cleanup, and people are still cleaning it up today.

A lot of people today, in their own families or work places or even churches, are careless in their euphoria but calculating in their violation. Some of us both celebrate God and use other people— simultaneously! With the best of intentions, we are capable of manipulating, persuading, and cajoling folks to help us meet *our* objectives rather than empowering them to conquer *theirs*. We have to reckon with the possibility that this might describe our behavior. This whole book has been about storms, but it's taken until the end, in a chapter about what happens *after the storm,* for us to come face-to-face with the possibility that we might just be the storm instead of the victim. Through our carelessness or our disrespect, we might be making the mess that somebody else will have to clean up. It could be that you've been reading all along, thinking about all the storms others are going through, but you've failed to recognize that when it comes to your inner circle, *you* are the storm.

Is it possible that you've been careless in your actions and attitudes? Is it possible that you've violated the trust of others, even those closest to you? Is it possible that others experience you like an EF5 tornado, wreaking havoc, wrecking relationships, causing all kinds of damage and leaving all kinds of mess behind you...mess that other people have to clean up?

Your family.
Your office.
Your church.

Pause for a moment and ask yourself honestly whether someone else has to put the cloak on their shoulders and walk backwards without looking to clean up a mess you made. Who has to play Shem and Japheth to your Noah or Ham?

Today, as we look at what happens *after the storm,* I long for you to take a personal inventory, look in the mirror, and ask yourself this question: **Who has to clean up after me?**

For some, Noah's experience hits very close to home. Alcohol is the deal for them. That was the case for a man I once heard of who was walking erratically on a city street at 1:00 A.M. A police officer spotted him and asked where he was going that time of night.

"Officer," he replied, "I am going to a lecture about alcohol abuse and the effects it has on the human body."

The officer said, "Really? Who is giving that lecture in the middle of the night?"

"My wife," the man answered.

We may laugh at jokes like this, but the reality for some is that it's

WHO HAS TO CLEAN UP AFTER ME?

no laughing matter. Maybe that's the reality you're living in. Alcohol is a problem, and you've got the DUIs to prove it. You keep saying, "I've got it under control," but you don't; it has *you* under control. Just like Noah, the wine or beer or liquor makes you and your family vulnerable to a mess that someone else will have to deal with later on.

A popular car website lists the legal blood alcohol level for driving in various countries, as well as some of the extraordinary penalties for drunk driving around the world. According to that report, if someone is convicted of a DUI in Malaysia, that person's spouse has to serve the jail time with them.[1] That sounds extreme and unfair, but in a way the same thing happens everywhere. In the United States, it's not formally written into the law that a spouse of a drunk driver will suffer, but it's the lived reality nevertheless. Seldom does someone's excessive drinking damage only that person. Al-Anon is a support program for those who have been affected by someone else's drinking problem. It helps people clean up the mess in their lives that was created by alcoholic parents, spouses, siblings, and children. I know a lot of people who are in this program. And I know a lot of others who have put someone in it. *Who has to clean up after me?*

For others, the issue looks more like Ham's offense than Noah's drunken stupor.

It's a sad truth that some people violate the trust and decency of those they should love the most. They leave their mate for someone else … and wonder why their kids don't just love their new boyfriend or girlfriend. Actually, the kids are just trying to clean up after the mess the adults have made. They just needed to be kids, and all of a sudden they've got all these grown-up cleaning responsibilities to take on. Or maybe the offense has little or nothing to do with sex and romance but everything to do with one's temper. Someone's family cleans up the dishes that they break, and it symbolizes for them the way they must clean up their souls and spirits from that person's latest tantrum. And maybe things would change if they could just stop and ask themselves, *Who has to clean up after me?*

Of course, there will be people who don't belong in either of these categories because neither alcohol abuse nor betrayal of others' trust is much of a problem. But we can make messes in many other ways, which those around us will have to clean up just as well.

> We buy impulsively…and our spouse has to clean up the credit.

> We gossip recklessly…and our church has to clean up the hurt feelings.

> We mistreat the environment…and our children will have to clean up the air and water.

It happens even among pastors in The United Methodist Church, where historically pastors have moved around every few years. Certain pastors are legendary for making messes in churches, and if you happen to be the next pastor, you might as well get out the mop! We all have it within us to create a storm for other people, to leave behind a mess that someone else will have to clean up. It could be as dramatic as a drug addiction or as seemingly innocent as a bit of gossip. Our actions rarely affect only us. And all of us need to stop and ask the hard question of ourselves: *Who has to clean up after me?*

So many others know all too well how true this is, that our actions can create problems for those closest to us. Why? Because they have been the child, spouse, sibling, coworker, or friend walking backwards with a garment on their shoulders, taking the tentative, awkward steps of fixing what others have caused to go wrong. Some of them have even been doing it so long that it's become almost second nature; the backwards walk has become a regular habit. That's why there's a flip side to the question of *Who has to clean up after me?* We also owe it to ourselves to ask, *Who am I cleaning up after, and should I be doing it?*

Whether you are a mess-maker or a mess-cleaner—and chances are you're a little bit of both—mark my words: The cleanup continues for generations! That's what Genesis 9 is all about; it sets in motion an intergenerational conflict that's still in motion even today.

WHO AM I CLEANING UP AFTER, AND SHOULD I BE DOING IT?

We all know it's true: Things really do run in families. I come from a family full of people who are simultaneously know-it-alls *and* chronic avoiders. We know everything about every subject, and there's no difficult conversation we can't put off until later! Maybe yours is the same. In fact, maybe your family dinners are so full of talk about issues that you never discuss emotions. Dwelling on current issues becomes the perfect cover for avoiding emotions. Everyone knows where you stand on presidential politics, but no one knows the wounds you've nursed since childhood. And the same story repeats all around the family dinner table; each person there has become adept at not asking what's going on in the others' hearts. Is that the way it is in your home? *Who cleans up after all of you?*

Those family patterns are inevitable, but they're not ironclad. With God's help, they can be broken. Some of my greatest joys in ministry happen when I see people break the harmful cycles in which they were raised.

I've seen sons of philanderers stay faithful.
I've seen daughters of addicts stay sober.
I've seen children of atheists come to faith.

Bad stuff runs in families... until by the grace of God it doesn't.

BAD STUFF RUNS IN FAMILIES, UNTIL BY THE GRACE OF GOD IT DOESN'T.

I have a glorious hope for the people of Good Shepherd Church and those who read this book. I hope that someday soon, you'll be able to ask yourself that question, *Who has to clean up after me?* and you'll be able to answer, *Now, at last, no one needs to.*

Questions for Reflection and Discussion

Write responses and other thoughts in the space below each question. If you are discussing the book in a small group, prepare for the meeting by writing answers in advance.

1. How does the story of Noah's drunkenness influence your view of Noah's legacy?

2. How did Noah punish Ham for his offense? Do you think the punishment was appropriate? Why or why not?

3. Do you know someone who was a Category 5 hurricane in your life or in the lives of people you know?

4. What was the situation, and how did you or the people involved respond to it?

5. What pain or difficulty did it cause?

6. How did you or others recover?

7. Name some ways that people cause storms in the lives of the ones they love without meaning to do so. What steps can people take to avoid causing lasting harm?

8. What are some storms you've caused? What storms are you currently causing?

9. What characteristics, good or bad, run in your family?

10. Have you seen someone break a cycle of bad behavior that they may have inherited?

11. What enabled them to overcome it?

12. How does this give you hope in your life or in the lives of those around you?

13. How do actions and consequences pass from one generation to the next? What examples can you give of someone making a mess that those who follow them will spend decades cleaning up?

14. Name one thing this week you will do to clean up after yourself so that someone else won't have to.

Ask Around

This week, identify three people in your inner circle, people whom you trust to give you an honest answer. Explain the message of this chapter to them, then ask them the question "What's it like to clean up after me?"

Alternatively, if you're studying this book in a small group, spend a few minutes asking the question of each other during your weekly meeting. Commit to praying for one another, asking God to help each group member to be sources of calm in the lives of their family and friends.

Closing Prayer

God, we know that our actions affect not only ourselves but also our loved ones and those around us. Help us to be aware of the ways we cause storms in the lives of our neighbors, as well as the ways in which others have to clean up after us. Give us courage to be honest and thorough as we look into our hearts and lives. Give us eyes to see clearly where we need to do better. And give us strength and guidance as we seek to become sources of calm. Amen.

Daily Scripture Readings

This week, read the following Scripture passages. Notice how the characters create messes for those around them to clean up. What lessons can you draw from their experience?

Monday: Genesis 3:1-24; 9:1-29
Tuesday: Judges 13:1-25
Wednesday: Judges 14:1-20
Thursday: Judges 15:1-20
Friday: Judges 16:1-31

1. From *http://jalopnik.com/this-map-will-show-you-drunk-driving-limits-all-over-th-1465013053*.

Where will your journey take you next?

CONVERGE
Bible Studies—
where topics and Scriptures merge,
transforming Christian lives.

9781426795534   9781426789533   9781426771576

Visit your local book retailer to see the complete list of Converge Bible Studies.

Published by

Other Studies
by Talbot Davis

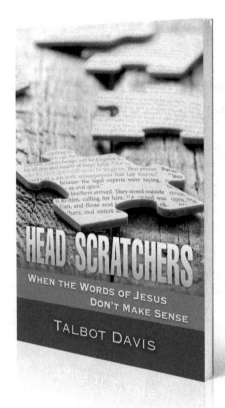

9781501802881

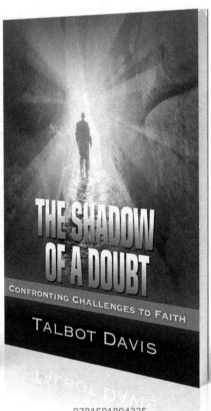

9781501804335

Order your copies today and continue studying with Davis.

Published by

CPSIA information can be obtained
at www.ICGtesting.com
Printed in the USA
LVHW032135060619
620439LV00005B/17/P